Wondrous
PLACES *of the* HEART

Alternative Therapy
with Children

Christine Alisa, MS

Wondrous Places of the Heart
Copyright © 2016 by Christine Alisa

Cover Design by Melodye Hunter

ISBN: 978-1944177-04-1 (p)
ISBN: 978-944177-05-8 (e)

Crescendo Publishing, LLC
300 Carlsbad Village Drive
Ste. 108A, #443
Carlsbad, California 92008-2999

www.CrescendoPublishing.com
GetPublished@CrescendoPublishing.com

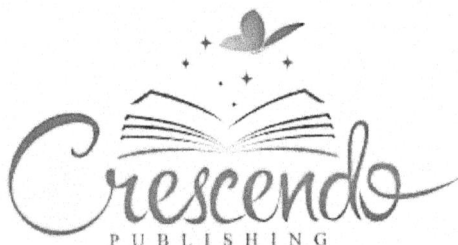

A Message from the Author

https://youtu.be/ACVclp5nTpg

To help you get the most out of my book, I have provided some complimentary bonus material including informative and educational audios and videos.

You can download all of these items at:
http://christinealisa.com/WPBook.html

People Love Wondrous Places
of the Heart

"This book is a solid guideline for parents with children in problems. It has a treasure of information about burdens that cause altered behavior in children. It outlines how to proceed and guide children through periods of suffering to become healthy and happy adults. A must-read for families looking for alternative insight and approach."

-Marc Van Hecke
Regression and P.L. therapist, Belgium

"I am very thankful that Christine has written this book in such a clear and understandable way. It gives direct usable information for both parents and professionals. Since I do not have time to read through thick books of theories, I was happy that in every chapter there is a clear structure. Each chapter subject contains explanations, experiences, and examples of cases describing how a child and their support system can be helped to deal with the problems. Most important of all she again made a clear connection with the heart. Very practical! "

Anita Groenendijk
MSc Environmental Sciences, Regression Therapist

"Through her wide range of methods Christine helps children release anxieties and fears. Christine uses both a fun and respectful approach with children. In a playful

way she gives them the opportunity to share their stories, while fully trusting the children and respecting their boundaries. This book is a great read for parents, teachers, therapists and other people that work with children. The focus is on empowering the children and help them regain strength and confidence."

-*Janine Booij*
Therapist and Life Coach

Contents

Introduction

My purpose for writing this book is twofold. I want to reach parents who are looking for more holistic ways to help their child or adolescent as well as acquaint those parents with my alternative approach to therapy. There seems to be a trend in our information-rich global atmosphere to lean more toward "out of the box" philosophies. People are getting fed up with the status quo and are taking charge of their own health and well-being. The same is true for parents raising children in this changing world. The old structures are not meeting the needs of our young people, so it is time for a change. My innovative therapeutic techniques bring about positive radical change and have the potential to improve the lives of children and families that experience my process.

While I have been on this planet, two of my passions have been to heal children's old wounds and help parents be the very best they can to support and nourish their families. I have witnessed such beautiful growth within those families as they navigate great challenges. It is my intention to familiarize others with the process I have developed to treat children and adolescents and to introduce the wondrous places of the many hearts that have touched me. Those resilient children and their families who have courageously walked a different path of therapy are the heart center of my work.

The majority of the chapters have a topic and within that topic I have included overviews of each issue highlighted along with case studies that show how my work has helped these children. There are indicators, warning signs, descriptions, and important aspects of each spotlighted area of concern, ranging from self-worth to physical abuse. There are also helpful solutions for parents at the end of each chapter along with resources that address specific problems that children experience.

In the words of one parent:

> I would like to let everyone know about this incredible woman, mentor, teacher, guide I am so blessed to have in my life and in my family's life. ... I realized just how far Christine stood out from the rest of the psychotherapy establishment. Her techniques, which may seem unorthodox to many (even to me in the beginning), seem so "spot-on" that I can't imagine doing it any other way. In this day and age finding a good therapist is a tremendous task. ... Finding someone in the category of Christine is almost impossible. Christine has been doing this amazing work for over twenty-five years. She is kind and generous with her time and energy. I can't say enough about this amazing woman. D. Clear

Chapter 1
My Alternative Therapeutic Healing Approach with Children and Adolescents

Have you been looking for an alternative type of therapy to help your child?

Have you tried traditional therapy for your child and your family without getting the results your child needed?

Have you ever heard of regression therapy?

Do you have an interest in other healing modalities?

The process that I developed to work with children and adolescents originated from my education, training, and the innovations I have created. However, throughout my career my personal work has been the catalyst for my therapeutic discoveries with children, adolescents, and their families. It all began when I was an elementary school teacher. At the time I was a teacher there was much greater freedom in the school system to teach to the "whole" child. I loved the children and the creativity that I could express at the time. However, I had a boy in my sixth-grade class who had been traumatized when he witnessed his father shooting and killing his mother. He did not seem to be responding to the counseling services the school provided, and his behavior was often disruptive and out of control. One day I sat him down after school and asked him what I could do to help him. He just shrugged. He was in so much pain. At that point I knew I had to find a way to help children like him. So I went to graduate school and subsequently became a Marriage Family Therapist.

Gestalt Therapy with Children and Adolescents:

I was very fortunate during the time of my therapist training to meet Violet Oaklander, PhD, who taught classes at the counseling center where I was an intern. She had written a book called *Windows to our Children,* which was about Gestalt therapy with children and adolescents. I immersed myself in her trainings and learned her therapeutic techniques. Pretty soon my therapy office was full of sand trays, shelves full of sand-tray figures, clay, paints, various art supplies, puppets, games, and dress-up clothes for dramatic play.

The Gestalt approach to therapy with children allows the child to manipulate materials and connect with them as they "speak" for a puppet, a clay figure, a drawing, or a sand-tray figure the feelings they have deep inside. I used her method to engage the child to dialogue with me through these mediums as I spoke or role-played the other sand tray or figures, puppets or drawings. The role-playing type of method is part of the Gestalt therapy process that grants children the safety they need while expressing their own feelings. Honoring the child's resistance and need for respect enables me to develop a relationship with the child while making contact with the child's inner and outer self. I recommend to the parents of the children I work with that they read Dr. Oaklander's book because it is filled with ideas on how to help children.

Regression Therapy:

Then my personal and professional journey took a turn. I had a wise therapist once who said that the more I worked on myself in my own therapy the better therapist I would become with my clients. I have tried to follow that advice throughout my career. Many healers have helped me on my journey to free myself of old wounds. One day my chiropractor that had helped me through four car accidents said that I needed to see a past-life therapist because she saw me sinking farther down into depression. So I began to see Dr. Morris Netherton who helped me unblock my suppressed childhood traumas. I had repressed incidents that were lying dormant in my unconscious. After a substantial amount of time spent uncovering my own issues, I began to take his classes and learned how to be a past-life therapist, or regression therapist as it is sometimes called. I became certified as "Master Therapist and Teacher" in the Netherton Method of Past Life Therapy. I found that I had an ability to not only help adults through the traumas of their early lives, but I could train other therapists as well.

Regression therapy helps people release old negative patterns that are impacting their lives and their relationships by accessing the unconscious messages that cycle around in the body and mind. I find the source of the blocks that are keeping people stuck, anxious, or depressed. I use a form of hypnosis to focus people into a light trance or altered state of consciousness, much like that feeling right before you go to sleep. By asking the deeper mind, the unconscious mind, to talk, I ask the client to locate a particular fear and the part of the body that is holding that fear. They end up finding the causes of phobias, illnesses, anger issues, or stuck patterns in their relationships, i.e., behaviors they repeat that drive their partner away.

Regression therapy works very effectively with people, and they do not have to believe in it. I tell parents that they do not have to believe in past lives for the process to work for them. I explain it as metaphor—something that feels very much like what we are feeling, something similar. Regression therapy helps people feel the emotions that have been stuffed down inside them. These buried emotions can affect the body in several ways. Scientists have told us that emotions and illness are connected, and when we do not deal with a painful emotion, the brain will react by triggering a specific illness in the body associated with that buried emotion. On the happy side, if the emotion is dealt with, the brain will trigger a mechanism for healing that organ. So regression therapy helps keep us healthy.

Regression Therapy with Children and Adolescents:

I have dedicated a portion of my private practice to working with children and adolescents. I wanted to see if I could combine in some way the Gestalt therapy with the regression therapy so that I could help the children in the same profound ways I was helping the adults in my practice. I started to develop what is now my storytelling technique that I write about in more detail in my book *Turning the Hourglass: Children's Passage Through Traumas and Past Lives.*

In the chapters of this book, you will read case studies of children who have benefited from my alternative approach to healing children and adolescents. I combined the therapeutic process of Dr. Oaklander's work with a gentle regression approach, which now forms the basis of my work with children and adolescents. It has proven to be an innovative, dynamic therapy that helps children make radical changes in their lives. Included family members become the receivers of the healing as well because I also conduct individual sessions with parents.

I train therapists internationally to do this work with children, and it is my goal to reach as many other therapists as possible that are drawn to the delightful healing experience with children and adolescents.

Shamanism as Part of My Healing Modality:

One day after I had just conducted a past-life regression session with an eighteen-year-old boy, I developed a headache that I couldn't "shake." It would not go away. After a Reiki session that I had, the practitioner said there was something attached to my head, and she recommended that I go to see a shamanic practitioner. What I found in that shamanic session was a spirit attachment that had been connected to the eighteen-year-old and had "jumped" onto me, so to speak. I was carrying that spirit attachment. Because I was both fascinated by the deep feelings that I resonated with during the session and relieved of the headache, I decided to train to become a shamanic practitioner myself. I learned the healing interventions and gained a deep connection to my own helping spirits during this phase of my life.

Shamanism is the earliest spiritual practice known to mankind and is practiced in many places around the world. "Shaman" is a Siberian word for healer though there are various traditions of shamanism throughout places such as Peru, Australia, and Europe that share common practices. In the United States the Native Americans' medicine man or woman is a more familiar concept.

One of the healing practices of shamanism is what shamans call extraction of spirit attachments. According to Steven D. Farmer, "Names for spirit attachments are" psychic intrusion, spiritual parasite, toxic energy, a psychic dart, or a curse." Whatever term is given to this or whatever its origin, it's not physical; however, if it remains in the individual's spiritual body, the risk is that it could manifest as a physical symptom or illness. Not all spirit attachments have a negative intention for us. They may be deceased relatives or ancestors who want to stay close to the person they loved while on Earth.

However, we all need our boundaries, whether they be physical, spiritual, or energetic, so shamans remove these attachments by extracting them. As a shamanic practitioner I remove attachments from children and adolescents as part of my alternative methods to heal the child. None of the spirit extraction work that shamanic practitioners do is meant to scare us; it's meant only to open up our energy fields in a loving way with the help of helping spirits like power animals.

I feel that helping the whole child—his mental, physical, emotional, and spiritual self—is the basis for my effective therapeutic approach. In both my own personal growth journey and my career, I have incorporated that belief into my own experience. Each child has a story. Each family has a path. Each human has a purpose. Freeing ourselves from the bonds of the past opens us to the joys of our relationships and our time here on Earth.

All the work that I do with children and adolescents is done with the intention of being for the greatest good. I do not re-traumatize them, but rather I unglue the past— much like deprogramming. I spend time with the parents explaining what I do and helping them to improve their relationships with their child or adolescent.

Chapter 2
Self-Worth

Is your child overly defensive?

Does your child have a hard time expressing themself?

Is your child self-critical, or does your child doubt themself?

Does your child often compare him/herself with others?

Does your child "cut" or engage in self-mutilation?

Definition of Self-Worth:

In our society we use *self-worth*, *self-esteem*, and *self-confidence* interchangeably because they essentially mean the same thing. How a child feels about him/herself is at the core of self-worth. Children have challenges to "belong" and feel accepted by others, whether that be peers, teachers, parents, or significant adults in their lives. Some children become people pleasers to satisfy that longing to be loved and accepted. Others act out and "test" the adults to see if they are really loved and accepted. Abraham Maslow, a humanist psychologist, created a hierarchy of needs for all people. They are physiological needs, safety and security needs, love and belonging needs, and esteem needs. According to Maslow, "We have two levels of esteem. One is respect of others, the need for status, recognition, attention and appreciation. The other is self-respect, competence, confidence and independence." When those needs are not met, or when they are disturbed in some way, self-esteem is diminished.

Warning Signs of Low Self-Worth in Children:

There are several indicators that a child may have low self-worth or low self-esteem (as we often call it). Some of these warning signs appear when a child or adolescent:

Avoids doing a task or does not want to try for fear of failure or frustration

Quits a game or activity without finishing it

Always wants to win

Has difficulty accepting praise

Withdraws from others and struggles with keeping friends

Constantly apologizes

Whines

Tries to please others but often feels empty inside if the pleasing doesn't work

Makes self-critical statements, e.g., "I'm ugly. I'm dumb."

Is easily influenced by peers to use or abuse drugs

Makes excuses for himself

Appears withdrawn and shy

Blames others

Lacks motivation

How Young Children Develop Self-Worth:

In all the years that I have seen children in therapy, I have discovered that their self-worth (or what I would rather call "sense of self") has been negatively affected. Whatever the issue was that brought him/her to therapy, there was often a disturbance in that sense of self. Whatever injuries occur within a child, those emotional or physical difficulties disrupt a child's sense of safety, which challenges their belief in themselves.

The center of a young child's life is their parent(s). The parent "mirrors" for the child who he/she really is. When a parent looks into the eyes of a baby with love and adoration, the baby sees him/herself as the object of that love and believes that is who he is. During this crucial bonding experience, not only are the child's physical needs being met, but the emotional needs are as well.

If there are disruptions in this process, like an alcoholic mother who neglects the infant's needs, survival patterns start to manifest. The child may learn that there is an inconsistency of love and attention. Fear develops in the child, which disturbs his/her sense of self, i.e., who he is. A child only knows to fill in the blanks when he/she is confused or denied his/her needs. He/she does not understand why something is happening, but he/she can put the blame on herself: *I must have done something wrong, or there is something wrong with me if my needs are not being met.*

Warning Signs of Low Self-Worth in Adolescent Behavior:

Adolescents are susceptible to low self-esteem because their lives change so much as they go through puberty. Learning to live in their changing bodies, finding friends to create peer bonding and acceptance, and being plagued by daily mood shifts are fodder for self-doubt. Some teens are so disconnected from their own feelings that they try behaviors to try to settle themselves.

Cutting

One behavior that is becoming more and more common is cutting. I have found that teens self-injure themselves for a variety of reasons. Adolescents who cut often do it to "feel," i.e., to feel that they are alive. Sometimes their depression is so deep inside them that cutting is the only way they can feel that they are truly alive. Their impulse to shut down in reaction to all the difficult experiences in their lives takes over so much, and they can't tolerate the numbness. If you know a teenager who is "spaced out," it is clearly a coping mechanism to filter out the bombardment of information that they cannot process. Teens are rapidly exposed to a large amount of input, but they have an undeveloped brain and maturity level, making them unable to manifest good choices. They often need to feel physical pain to restore their belief that they are truly here. Their feeling of invincibility makes cutting even more appealing. "How far can I go now before I truly kill myself?"

I also see cutting as a way for some teens to call attention to some pain that is unconscious in them. It is a way to "tell" the adults that something is wrong, that "I need some help." Teens who are suicidal may choose cutting as the first behavior that indicates how close they are to killing themselves. Or they call attention to another pain, such as family problems, reactions to divorce, peer difficulties, and lack of an ability to express themselves with words. Adolescents who hold in things are susceptible to cutting. They either have no one they can really talk to safely, or they do not want to open up to the emotions that are swirling around them. Emotions can be painful and confusing in adolescents, and cutting is a solution that distracts them from the real pain.

Then there are other teenagers I see in therapy who clearly want to be dramatic and imitate their friends who cut. I have heard, "Everybody does it" from teens in my office. There is almost a cultural draw or rite of passage they feel when they cut. I believe in our culture we have lost track of the profound need adolescents have for some kind of rite-of-passage ceremony into adulthood. Other cultures or some religions have a process or test to move a child into adulthood, but we lack anything deep and connected to that spirit in our society as a whole. When girls start their periods, it is not usually thought of as a positive experience. However, it can be an opportunity for girls to connect with the woman they are becoming; it can be a way to honor this time in their life, to celebrate it.

What is a "sense of self"?

In her book *Windows to our Children,* Violet Oaklander, PhD, talks about the child's sense of self. She says:

> When I see a child in therapy, I have the opportunity to give her self back to her, for in a sense a poor self-concept is a lost sense of self. I have a chance to bring her in touch with her own potency, to help her feel at home in the world. ... In regaining her sense of self, she can then throw herself fully into the process of exploring and discovering all the things in her world.

In my work with children, one of my goals is to help bring back their sense of self. Awareness of their body and body image are important aspects of accepting themselves. I often ask the children to draw themselves, and they tell me about the drawing. When children identify their characteristics, strengths, and weakness to me, they become closer to feeling a sense of self—not how they wish they could be, but who they really are. I provide activities that nurture their senses: touching, seeing, hearing, smelling, and sometimes tasting. One of the children's favorites is what I call "Oogla." It is a mixture of cornstarch, water, and tempera paint. The children put their hands into the mixture, and we create stories together about their fears, dreams, and experiences. We use the body to do movement games, dramatic play, toy sword playing, and even playing with toys in a container of water. These experiences bring the child back to him/herself and the sense of self.

Case Study:

When Michael came to me for therapy, he was eight years old. He was a very bright boy who was isolated at school with no friends. He took on the feelings of others and was an adult people pleaser. He was very torn inside because his parents had divorced when he was three years old, and his life totally changed after that. His father moved away, and he lived with his mother and two sisters, seeing his father on vacations. His father brought him to therapy on one of his visits to determine if the custody agreement was really working for Michael. It clearly was not, so I recommended that he be able to stay with his father (whom he missed terribly) to determine if it should be a permanent place for him. Both parents agreed, and I began to see Michael for sessions on a regular basis.

Michael is a gentle, sensitive boy who harbored a lot of empathic feelings toward others. He had a tendency to take on others' pain, hence making it more difficult for him to work with his own feelings. He did not want to feel angry because then he envisioned himself as an aggressive person, which he was not. He loved both his parents, and did not want to hurt either one of them by choosing who he wanted to live with. He was an intelligent boy who was creative and liked to write. However, he had difficulty falling asleep at night and sometimes cried himself to sleep. Michael was a very good kid who did not act out but rather kept his feelings inside.

Things were going well in therapy, and he was allowing some of his anger to be released around the divorce. He wanted more time with his father, so we had sessions with the father, which improved the father-son relationship. Then his parents made arrangements for his mother to move closer to his father and stepmother. The mother had been living in another state, so it had been difficult for Michael. He missed one parent while he was with the other. At first, this arrangement seemed wonderful until issues with his little sister erupted. The parents had different parenting styles, which complicated things for

Michael. His sister would be out of control at his mother's house, and she aggravated him most of the time.

Michael started feeling more and more pressure in his life. He had been accepted in the GATE program for gifted children at his school, but found the extra work they gave him overwhelming. He worried about his mother, who did not have a job. Emotional issues started to manifest themselves in his body, which, of course, is common when working with children. They hold their feelings in their body. However, I decided to work with these physical complaints by finding their source in Michael's earlier experiences.

He came to therapy one day reporting that he had a pain above his eye and said he couldn't see well in his left eye. I used my regression therapy techniques with children by asking him what emotion was coming from the pain in his eye. He was able to determine that it was shock that his dad was leaving. His mother was crying and telling his dad not to leave. Michael felt confused, abandoned, sad, helpless, and angry in this difficult moment in his young life. He was remembering the incident, and the cells in his eye held the emotions that needed to be released. When children feel confused, I help them go "under" the confusion instead of letting it take over. He felt better after the session.

Michael's unconscious mind and his body became his road map to the issues that were lying dormant inside him. He told me in the following session of a nightmare he had where he woke up with his head buzzing and he felt scared. I asked him to "go to where this scared feeling is coming from." He found a scene where he was four years old and was being babysat by his thirteen-year-old sister. She was very angry, screaming at him, and tried to tie him to his bed. He described her anger as "uncontrolled." He said he was "falling on a bed in a room." I asked him, "What is making you fall on a bed?" He answered, "I'm being dropped by my big sister onto a bunk bed." I went on to ask him, "What is making you feel dizzy?" He answered, "A rope is around me, and I fall to the floor, pass out, fall asleep, and then she comes back. She is saying that she hates me." His mother came into the room and began arguing with her daughter. His sister was resorting to anger and out-of-control behavior that scared Michael. He had trouble expressing anger himself because those around him had little or no control of their own.

I often tell parents that it sometimes gets worse before it gets better in therapy. What that means is the child may regress in behavior to a younger age or display behaviors and symptoms on a more regular basis. After doing this deeper work with children and adults for many years, I know that the body is just trying to tell us what to clear next. We are listening to the body now, and the body is "talking to us." Michael told me about physical pain in his head, neck, and right jaw. He said, "It feels like there's a big hammer inside my head."

I chose to work with Michael's birth at this point. His mother had told me earlier that Michael's birth was an emergency C-section. How a child handles stress often begins in birth, and Michael was dealing with a lot of stress in his life. It turned out that the birth was a long, painful process for his mother and himself. The birth had started and then stopped. He appeared to be coming out breach, and the cord was wrapped around his foot. His mother was very angry and upset that she could not have a natural birth and needed drugs. Michael had drugs in his system, which had created the dizzy feeling. I had him breathe together with me to breathe out the drugs. The pattern in his birth was that he had to go through pain before he came alive.

I helped Michael release a lot of anger in my office. I have a big bear in my office that he would punch to his heart's desire. It was my observation that Michael stored his feelings in his head, and I wanted to make sure I found the source of that anger in the places he needed to go in his past. His parents decided to have him undergo an MRI to find out if there was anything physically wrong. The doctors found nothing.

Michael had a breakthrough session one day while we were making scenes in the sand tray. As he made his scene, I made mine. He had been talking to me about how he felt that his mother was not listening to him. She didn't seem to understand him. He talked about the pain in his head feeling like a knife or a bullet skimming his head and making a cut, so I started a story, asking him to help me. He told me, "A man is running into the woods because people with guard dogs are after him. He trips and goes unconscious. He climbs a wall-like fence and gets to a building that's locked." I asked him, "Is this building familiar or unfamiliar to you?" He said, "It's familiar."

Then he said, "I think I figured it out. The building is my mom's house. The fence is what's keeping me from getting there. She's not able to understand what I'm saying, and I'm not able to understand what she says. Then the dogs are what is causing that fence to be there, and the people are doing the same thing as the dogs. I mean the dogs are the things that are part of my mom and me. This dog (he points to a dog figure in the sand) could be part of me causing me to not understand my mom, and this other dog (he points to another dog figure) can't understand me." I said, "When these dogs are forcing the man over the fence, is the fence like a wall?" He responded, "Yes, like a soundproof wall." He put a figure of a person representing himself in the sand on one side of the wall and a figure of his mom on the other side.

Michael's revelation about his and his mother's communication was awe-inspiring because he found his own understanding of what was going on in his life. It gave him a great sense of confidence in himself. His ability to see the similarity through this story was lovely. He was experiencing one of those "aha" moments, and it was a pleasure to witness it. He was able to see that it was both his mother's and his issues that were keeping them from communicating with each other. Whether this story is a past-life or a metaphor for Michael's life, the awareness that he discovered from the experience was priceless. We subsequently scheduled sessions to work on the communication between him and his mother.

When Michael finished therapy with me, he was focusing better in school with fewer behaviors looking like ADHD. He had more friends and participated in sports. Michael learned to express his feelings better rather than bury them all in headaches. He had been such a people pleaser, taking on other people's feelings, but he told me one day, "Now I'm not other people's punching bag anymore." He stood up for himself, but more importantly he knew his boundaries—where he began and the other person began. He had found his sense of self.

Solutions:

Communication Strategies:

Listen to, acknowledge, and accept the child/adolescent's feelings.

Use "**I**" messages when speaking to your child. "**I** am bothered that you didn't finish your homework on time."

Be **honest**.

Respect his/her feelings and needs.

Involve him/her in problem-solving situations that **involve** the child's life.

Avoid "should" and **repetitive** "advice."

If children say something negative about themself, **try not to contradict them.** (For example, when they say, "I am so dumb," don't say, "No, you are so smart." This only reinforces their negative feeling. Children start believing they are wrong to think that they are not smart. Just allow the bad feelings to be expressed. Listen to their feelings.)

Talk to your son or daughter about **school pressures**, including the need to conform as well as peer pressure, and let them express feelings to you.

Guidelines for Parents to Enhance Their Child's Sense of Self:

Give your children **space** to learn how to manage their own lives.

Give your children **opportunities** to pursue their own interests.

Support their **uniqueness** even though it may be different from your own.

Take them seriously. **Do not discount** what they say or do.

If a situation like **a divorce** has happened, have your child **evaluated** by a therapist and find one for yourself as well.

If you discover your child or adolescent is **cutting,** talk to him/her about it without judgment. **Seek professional help**.

Notice what peer pressures your child/adolescent is experiencing. **Be aware** of **behaviors** or activities that his/her friends may be engaged in that are affecting your son or daughter negatively.

Quick Win Strategies:

- Allow your children to be who they really are even if it is different from you.

- Listen to your children's negativity toward themselves without correcting.

- Seek outside help if there is divorce or other changes in family life.

- If your child is cutting, seek out a therapist who specializes with children and adolescents.

Chapter 3
Anger

Do you have a child or teenager who is angry and acting out?

Does your child get in trouble at school for fighting?

Is your child taking out his/her anger on siblings at home on a regular basis?

Are you as a parent getting frustrated, trying to deal with your child's anger?

Why Children Experience Anger

Anger is a much more powerful feeling than fear, helplessness, or sadness. When a child experiences powerlessness, it builds up inside them, and over time, it comes out as anger. I tell kids all the time, "You are like a jar. When you hold a lot of feelings inside yourself like a jar, eventually the lid snaps off and you get angry. Then a lot of times you get in trouble."

If a child does not feel like they are being heard or listened to, they get noticed by getting angry. Sibling and peer disagreements, homework, and stresses in the home or at school are some of the causes of anger. In my therapy private practice I also see children who do not know why they are angry. We find the causes in the unconscious mind and then release them to be problem solved at a conscious level.

Anger versus Depression:

Children who are depressed are usually holding their anger inside and not expressing it. They also have experiences that have "shut them down," such as traumatic events, hurtful experiences, losses, and grief. When children's sense of self or self-esteem is diminished, they often feel depressed. When the depressed child can express his/her anger in a healthy way, he/she feels stronger and more open to the world. Children can be angry and depressed at the same time. It is just the anger we see, not the depression deep inside.

Case Study

When children come to me who are having difficulties in their lives, I often find that they are angry about various stresses in their life, such as a divorce, a change in the family, sibling disagreements, or difficulties with parents or friends. In these situations I provide a safe place for them to feel that anger because I encourage them to express it. I teach them how to release the anger so that they do not get in trouble. However, there are also cases where the anger is very deep-seated. It has little to do with the family dynamics and more to do with unconscious material from the child's past. The alternative therapy that I use, regression therapy, saved this boy and his family from what could have been a very destructive life.

Scott was a twelve-year-old boy who came to therapy because of his angry, often violent behavior. He would take out his anger on his younger brother by punching him. When his stepfather intervened to stop him, Scott would physically attack his father by kicking and punching him. He would slam the door to his bedroom so hard that it almost broke off the hinges. His temper would erupt with little provocation. Scott's family was not an abusive or violent one, but they felt helpless as to how to handle Scott's volatile outbursts. When his stepdad intervened to get control of the situation, Scott's mother would try to protect Scott in a codependent manner, thus undermining his stepdad.

The only childhood trauma that Scott appeared to have experienced was the abandonment of his biological father. Scott had had little contact with the man throughout his young life, but it did contribute to the distant feeling he had for his stepdad, who was the father of his younger brother. Scott had been diagnosed with ADD and a learning disability, which were also contributing factors to his anger. His parents did not want to give him medication for the ADD, but he was receiving special help at school for his disability.

Through regression therapy, Scott and I uncovered several past lives and a traumatic birth that contributed to his rage. Through the use of clay and the technique I have developed for resolving past issues, Scott found a past life where he had been a man who killed another man. He had shot the man in an act of revenge because he took his money. It was a sad story because the man he killed had been his best friend. I often ask children to tell me what they are feeling under the anger. We usually find helplessness, sadness, confusion, and/or fear, as was the case with Scott. In his rage he lost a good friend. Now he was reenacting this rage with his younger brother, whom he really loved, but Scott was being "driven" by the patterns of his past.

Scott also had an issue of feeling trapped, which I find common in children diagnosed with ADD. When his stepfather would hold him down to prevent him from hitting his brother, Scott was duplicating various places in his past where he had been trapped, one of which was his birth. The umbilical cord had been wrapped around his neck, and he felt scared that he was going to die. He felt stuck and trapped. The doctor conducted an emergency C-section to remove the cord. During the time his mother was drugged, he, the baby, couldn't "feel" his mother and thus became afraid. I have found that babies have both a physical experience and an emotional experience. When the mother is given drugs, babies feel the difference, like a void. We worked with this fear by doing a rebirth process—being born the way he would have liked to come alive—and he felt better.

Another impactful lifetime was one where he was in a gang and constantly fighting other gangs. Scott revealed that in that lifetime he went to jail and even fought in jail. It was all he knew—fighting to survive. The similarity to his life now was profound. I helped him to understand that the past is over, and he can make new choices. An integral part of the therapy for that period of time was the family therapy I conducted with all the members. Each one was hurting and needed to express the reality that was true for each one of them. I worked with the family on their communication to help them understand each other. At this point, Scott was doing better and the angry outbursts were gone, so his therapy was completed.

As often happens with a child, issues come up when he/she reaches a new developmental level. When Scott was fifteen years old, his parents brought him back to me again because he stole a relative's iPod and lied about it. The stealing experience originated from his feeling of being deprived of things that other people take for granted. He felt he was entitled to have things even when they weren't his. This irrational belief system became the focus of the next phase of our work together.

We used the sand tray to uncover a past life where he had been an orphaned beggar boy who had nothing. In that lifetime he was resentful of others who had things/food and he did not. He felt hopeless and ended up dying of starvation. Though Scott's parents gave him most things and he didn't want for much, they weren't ready to get him an iPod or iPhone, so he took it upon himself to take it. The lying is what bothered his parents so much—as it does most parents. He ended up giving the iPod to a fellow student and never got it back.

At the close of our work together, Scott took a more motivated interest in school, joined the wrestling team (where he excelled), and worked with his stepdad in his electrical business. Scott's self-esteem improved, and I got a note from his parents when he finished high school. Scott's gifts lay with what he could do with his hands—

his mechanical strengths, which had very little to do with traditional schooling. I am very proud of him.

Use of Regression Therapy with Children and Adolescents:

I have developed a process that I utilize with children and adolescents that I call my "storytelling technique," which includes Gestalt and regression therapy. I use this process to help children like Scott find the root causes of their negative behavior. Gestalt therapy helps children to "own" their feelings, not discount them. Regression therapy explores the unconscious mind where we have "recorded" past traumas that have created negative patterns. By telling these stories, children connect with the feelings deeply.

In all the years that I have worked with children, I have witnessed them expressing deep feelings and letting them go. As a result they are able to problem solve for themselves and gain confidence in the process. I always tell parents that you cannot ask a child to think if he has an emotional backpack on his shoulders. If we find a story that has the emotions the child connects to, he/she is able to feel and release. That story or metaphor is a gateway to understanding the internal anger that keeps the child unhappy.

Medication:

Many parents do not want to medicate their child for depression, anger, ADD, or ADHD. Some physicians prescribe antidepressants for children with anger issues, but I am a proponent of non-use of medication for the health of the child. In my opinion and experience, the side effects plus the addictive nature of medication leads to problems in adulthood.

Alternatives to medication are now available in health-food stores and through homeopathic doctors and naturopathic physicians. The elimination of foods that create allergic reactions in children and the use of food supplements can also be helpful. Treating the whole child with therapy and alternative medicine, I believe, is the direction of healthy conscious parenting.

Solutions:

Outlets for Anger

When I work with parents and children, I have a session where we talk about what to do when children get angry at home. If children have an **outlet**, they will have **better impulse control**. It is when the children do not express their feelings that they act impulsively. This is not about letting children get away with doing something wrong or spoiling them. It is about giving them **tools to work** out their own feelings. Here are some ideas:

Sit down and communicate with the child. **Listen** to their **feelings** and the feelings that might be **under the anger**, such as fear, hurt, and/or sadness.

Give the child/teen a **punching bag** to hit when something really makes them mad.

Have the child use a **whiffle bat** to hit a pillow. Do it with the child. Take turns. Parents get angry at things too!

Draw pictures of what color anger is. **Scribble** what anger looks and feels like for **younger children.**

Take some **ice,** put it in a strong plastic trash bag, get a **mallet** from the hardware store, and have your child smash the ice. Then put the **smashed ice** in a **drink** and enjoy.

Have the child practice tapping or **Emotional Freedom Technique** by using their fingers to **tap** the spots right below the collarbone as they say, "Even though I am really angry, I am still a cool kid." Do this until they **relax.** Children also can tap using the **karate chop** location on the side of their hand. See Nick Ortner's book for more information.

How to Communicate with Your Child

Avoid getting angry, raising your voice, or being defensive.

Notice if you are getting your **"buttons" pushed**. Don't react from that place.

Be present for your child. Stop what you are doing and pay attention.

If the anger is a reaction to a limit or boundary you set, let them verbalize their anger. If the issue is non-negotiable but you are **willing to listen** to his/her side, do so. You **might find out** something you didn't know before and there may be room for compromise.

Use **listening skills** where, for example, you might say, "You really are angry at Billy. He really hurt your feelings and you want him to feel like you do."

Remember to hear if there are other feelings **under the anger** and reflect that to your child. You do not need to agree with them; just validate their feelings.

Set aside some **one-on-one** time with your child/teen and create an activity that you both enjoy. It makes children/teens feel loved and valued. **Listen, laugh**, and **enjoy**.

There are some excellent books on communicating with your child and your teen. Read them for more in-depth information.

Family Therapy Communication:

When I work with families, I give them **exercises to improve their communication** with their child or teenager. One of the exercises that has proved very effective is based on speaking of things you **like and dislike**. There are always things we don't like about **each other's** behavior, and by creating a structured safe place to express those feelings, parent and child end up **feeling closer** after one of these sessions. This is how it works:

1. I ask the child to say one thing that they like about their parent or something the parent does that they like to the parent.

2. Then I ask the parent to say one thing that they like about their child or something the child does that they like to the child.

3. Then I ask the child to say one thing that they so not like about their parent or something the parent does that they do not like to the parent.

4. I ask the parent to say one thing that they do not like about their child or something the child does that they don't like.

5. Repeat another positive statement to each other.

6. Repeat another do not like statement to each other.

7. Continue for about six to ten times and see how you feel toward one another.

There is no discussion. There are only statements as you take turns. Do this a few times with different statements and notice how you feel toward one another.

Coping Strategies

- Provide outlets for your child's anger.

- Communicate with your child when they are angry.

- Provide therapy and alternatives to medication.

- Participate in family therapy.

BONUS: To discover more tips and strategies on how to deal with **anger**, attitude, and lack of responsibility with your teenager in a **productive** and **positive**

way, listen to my complimentary Q & A teleseminar on Communicating with your Teenager.

Get your BONUS CONTENT by going to the URL below:

http://christinealisa.com/WPBook.html

Chapter 4
Trauma

Has your child experienced something traumatic?

Was your child's birth traumatic?

Does your child seem to regress to an earlier age, e.g., start wetting the bed again?

Are you puzzled because there has been no traumatic experience in your child's life, but he/she has acute separation anxiety?

Definition of Trauma:

According to the American Psychological Association:

> Trauma is an emotional response to a terrible event like an accident, rape or natural disaster. Immediately after the event,

shock and denial are typical. Longer-term reactions include unpredictable emotions, flashbacks, strained relationships and even physical symptoms like headaches or nausea.

People undergo emotional shock as part of the experience of trauma. The characteristics of emotional shock include a shutting down of the body and mind; and feeling numb physically, mentally, and emotionally as a response to flight or fight, or reaction to stress. This emotional shock is the body's way of helping a child through trauma, but it leaves symptoms like depression and anxiety after the onset of the traumatic event.

Dr. Candace Pert explains in her book *Molecules of Emotion* that neurotransmitters called peptides carry emotional messages. "As our feelings change, this mixture of peptides travels throughout your body and your brain. And they're literally changing the chemistry of every cell in your body." I believe that the emotions that occur during times of trauma do lodge in the body as Dr. Pert describes. "The cells keep recreating the emotions so a child displays symptoms of trauma even when the trauma is over."

Types of Trauma

There are several types of trauma that children experience. They range from sudden experiences like dog bites, car accidents, death of a family member, earthquakes, fires, storms, and emergency C-section births, to the trauma the child experiences with physical, emotional, and sexual abuse. There are also long-term types of trauma that build up and can create the symptoms common to the more sudden incidents of trauma. Some prolonged types of trauma include parental addiction and neglect.

Birth Trauma:

One of the types of trauma that I have worked with over the years is birth trauma. A traumatic birth may include an emergency C-section, the umbilical cord being wrapped around the baby's neck, premature birth with prolonged time spent in the incubator, a life-death crisis with the mother, and even surgeries after the birth. These experiences create a reaction in the body and with the emotions. I work with the children to "lift" the effects of those births.

As a parent you might ask, "How does birth trauma affect my child's behavior, and why would it be an important piece of my child's therapy?" I answer parents by telling them that birth creates a stress pattern. A stress pattern is developed when there is fear, like fight or flight. If there has been any disturbance in the natural way a child wants to be born or a mother's well-being, a pattern appears. If there is a place in the birth where the child is "stuck," he/she can have a pattern similar to this: "When I go through things in my life, I usually feel stuck." All births have some sort of stress to them, and that is healthy. We all have stress, but it is the way we handle stress that can create difficulties in our lives.

More and more parents have had their babies through Cesarean births. According to the Centers for Disease Control and Prevention, "32.7% of all deliveries were Cesarean for 2013. The rates were slightly lower for 2012, but the rates have steadily been gaining since 1996 when they were 20.7% of all deliveries in the United States."

Cesarean births themselves are not necessarily traumatic if they are planned, but there are incidents where the family was hoping for a natural birth and the mother experienced placenta previa or placental abruption, and where the baby was premature or in a breech position and doctors recommended Cesarean.

Statistics for Birth Trauma:

Prevention and Treatment of Traumatic Childbirth cited that "between 25–34% of women report that their births were traumatic. A birth is said to be traumatic when the individual (mother, father, or other witness) believes the mother's or her baby's life was in danger, or that a serious threat to the mother's or her baby's physical or emotional integrity existed."

Case Study of Birth Trauma:

To illustrate how birth trauma can negatively affect children and the positive results that can be attained by my therapeutic process, I want to describe a case I had of a boy who was two and a half years old; I am calling him Marcos. He was brought to me for therapy because he was not functioning like children of his age. There was nothing wrong with him organically or developmentally; however, he was not talking, walking, or crawling correctly. He was using his elbows and arms to pull himself along. He cried a lot and seemed very sad. His parents were taking him to physical and speech therapy, but there had been few results.

When Marcos was born, his heart rate started dropping and he had respiratory problems, so the doctors performed an emergency Cesarean section. He had already been in the birth canal with the umbilical cord wrapped around his neck. After he was born, he was circumcised and had to stay in an incubator for nine days before he went home. At eighteen months, he had to go back to the hospital for a surgery because his testicle had not descended. Every time his parents took him to the doctor or the hospital, he would scream and cry.

In the first session I had with Marcos, I tried to play with him by rolling a ball back and forth to him. If the ball didn't go directly to him, he would make a crying sound and point for his mother to go get the ball for him. He did not want to move. He was irritable and sad-looking.

I used a combination of therapeutic techniques with Marcos to heal his traumatic wounds. I asked the parents to help me by holding him while I reenacted his birth in my sand trays using figures of mother, doctors, and baby, where the parents lovingly but firmly held him like in a cocoon, all the while telling him that he was safe now, that they loved him and it was all over. (When I work with the very young, I often ask the parent to stay in the room and sometimes participate in the therapy.)

I made scenes in the sand tray of Marco's birth, surgeries, and the time he spent in the incubator while he sat on his parents' laps looking at my "story." He cried and struggled in his parents' arms, trying to get down and away. His unconscious mind had held onto the negative scary experiences, which were not allowing him to flourish. It was my job to facilitate him moving through the experiences again but this time with love and safety. He was angry as I talked about being stuck in the canal and the doctors having to cut his mom's tummy to pull out the baby. I allowed his anger, and we all said we were angry too. His unconscious reaction to the act of "moving"—whether it be talking, walking, or crawling— had the pain and fear of being stuck in the canal (a painful experience) attached to it. So in his reality it was best not to move.

After a few weeks of therapy, he was smiling, trying to enunciate his words, crawling as fast as he could, trying to stand on his own, rolling the ball back and forth to his mom and me joyfully, and giving me "love taps." When he had to go to another doctor's appointment to have the other testicle surgically descended, he didn't cry. He was calm and responsive to the doctor, which overjoyed his parents.

Marcos went from being a sad, angry, almost immobile child who made little eye contact to a giggling, busy one, eager to learn to do all the physical things appropriate for his age. Clearing the birth issues helped Marcos reclaim his joy and loving feelings. I am so glad to share his happy ending here.

Behaviors of Children Who Have Experienced Trauma:

It is so hard as parents to witness our children experience something traumatic and not know what to do about their reactions. Each child behaves and reacts in their own way to trauma, but some of the things to look for include withdrawal, avoidance, anxiety, separation anxiety, phobias, frequent tantrums or "meltdowns," difficulty concentrating, wetting the bed, and angry outbursts. Their self-esteem may be affected, and they may not feel confident about themselves. Sometimes children have nightmares, which repeat and wake them up at night.

They may have fears about going to school or to a new place.

Some traumas are very clear to the parent. Maybe the child is scared to go to sleep because his/her grandmother has just passed away and the child does not understand death. Another child may not want to go in the car because he/she was in a car accident.

Other behaviors or symptoms may puzzle the parent because there does not seem to be a clear reason why the child has recurrent nightmares or is fearful and anxious. Those situations can have their source in early childhood trauma or past lives. I use my regression therapy techniques in those cases.

Case Study of Past-Life Trauma

In order for parents to have a clear understanding of how trauma can come directly from past lives, I will talk about a case of a twelve-year-old boy whose parents brought him to me. Previously Peter had been doing well in school and getting along with siblings, and he was generally happy. He came from a loving family, and there had been no traumatic event in his life.

Then everything changed. Peter would leave school projects to the last minute, and his grades dropped. He spent a lot of time on the computer and seemed to regress in his behavior. He wanted to play only with his much younger brother and not friends his age. He would cry if his mother left to go somewhere. He had regular nightmares and would wet the bed. He would ignore his mother when she asked him to do something—even come to dinner. He clung to his mother and ignored his father.

Immediately Peter responded to my storytelling technique of regression therapy. I told him that he could make what I call "scenes" in my sand trays. He proceeded to create three war scenes. One was the present war (one that was going on at the time). One was a future war using nuclear weapons, and one was a past war. He described the past war in detail with my help. He had been a soldier in a very long war in India at the time of the British occupation. When a cannon exploded, he was injured. His jaw and several other bones were broken. When he was treated at the temporary hospital, they wired his jaw shut. They gave him gas for the pain while they performed surgery. He wasn't able to scream because the enemy would know their location. When he was telling me how they cut his knee to remove some metal, he pointed to his own knee.

It was quite extraordinary how Peter was able to give such detail, not only about the war he described, but his injuries as well. When I asked him to speak for the soldier he became that soldier, feeling the injury and the weariness of war. At the end of the session, he was feeling sad, but he wanted to show his parents the scene he had made in the sand tray. The source of his trauma was the war and its negative impact on him physically and mentally.

We addressed his procrastination issue around schoolwork. I asked him how he felt about homework, and he said, "I do not want to do it. I feel helpless, lonely, and stuck." By asking him clear, concise questions to his unconscious mind, he told me about a lifetime where he was climbing Mount Everest. Then an avalanche forced him into a cave. He finally continued to climb through the freezing weather. However, he told me, "There are a lot of hardships." He found that he was off course. He and his comrades made an SOS sign in the snow after running out of food and fearing that they would die. He said, "His brain cells are frozen. He can't finish it. He was trying for a world record, but gave it up." It was like what he felt when he was doing his homework. When he stopped, he was afraid that he wouldn't get back to it. The fear of not surviving was like a blank spot in his unconscious mind. In that lifetime he was picked up by a plane and taken to a hospital where he recuperated, but he felt defeated and injured.

Through a few other sessions where he experienced trauma, Peter understood the dynamics of his past lives and how they fit into his current life. A prevalent theme for him was the idea that he didn't want to do what others wanted him to do. He had spent those former lives living the way others wanted him to live and doing what he thought was the honorable thing to do. Peter knew that he could now have his own feelings about things, instead of just rebelling against others. When he followed other people's rules and expectations, he had been hurt and suffered.

After those sessions Peter was happier, and his grades were high again. The nightmares ended, and he stopped wetting the bed. He listened to his mother and enjoyed his whole family. Even though his father wanted him to be very competitive in his tennis class, he chose to do the best he could and enjoy the game. His father and he enjoyed a closer relationship. He had let go of the heavy traumas of his past and was finding his way.

Effects of Ongoing Trauma Due to Parental Addiction and Subsequent Neglect:

We know that addiction is a problem that many adults struggle with on a daily basis. However, once parents take control of their lives and enter treatment and twelve-step programs, they can attend to the effects their own behaviors have had on their child. Children from these families suffer a kind of trauma that seems endless because of the day-to-day wondering if the parent is going to be sober or not and the inconsistency of when he/she will get their needs met.

Children who come from addicted families or who are left in the care of an addicted parent or guardian are usually depressed, withdrawn, and impulsive. Their ability to concentrate is diminished, and they can exhibit symptoms of mental illness. In my private practice I have hesitated to diagnose children with what are usually adult diagnoses like bipolar disorder or borderline personality disorder, but the child can show early signs of these disorders. In my experience I have seen teenagers, who would have developed one of these disorders by their early adulthood, be totally turned around by my therapy and their parents' intervention. Children and adolescents of addicted parents are at greater risk of becoming substance abusers themselves.

Solutions:

What a Parent Can Do to Help Their Traumatized Child:

Parents can help their child through a traumatic event by utilizing some of these suggestions at home or along with therapy:

Create safety and security in the home.

Tell your child he/she is **safe now** and that the event is over.

Comfort your child by **reading** a story/book that empowers children like There's a Nightmare in My Closet.

Sit down and communicate with the child. **Listen** to his/her **feelings without judgment**.

Ask them about their fears.

Refrain from criticizing them if they wet the bed or are overly afraid.

Comfort your child by cuddling and spending time with them.

Ask them **what they need** to feel free of the fear. **Validate** their response.

Empower your child by asking what they would like to do **to change their fear**.

Take your child to a **qualified therapist** who has experience with trauma.

Enter therapy as a parent to help you through the emotions you experience because you witnessed your child's trauma or simply know that your child has been traumatized.

If **addiction** is present in the home, enter a treatment program or join a twelve-step program like AA, NA, or Al-Anon.

If you have a belief system that the child is being watched over from above, **reassure your child** of that fact.

Drawing Tips:

Have them draw the **nightmare** or bad dream and tell you about it.

Draw pictures of the **traumatic event** and allow them to feel the pain, sadness, or fear. Have them share those feelings with you and comfort them.

Have them draw pictures of the traumatic event, **tear them up**, throw plastic darts at the picture, or **yell at the picture** to loosen its hold on the child.

Have your child draw pictures of where he/she **feels safe**. Put those pictures on the wall or refrigerator.

Draw a **picture** of that **fear** and tell it to go away. **Scribble** on it and rip it up.

Communication Strategies:

When children want to avoid the subject of the traumatic event, tell them that if they **hold in those feelings**, it will not get better. Talking about it may be painful, but you are there to listen **unconditionally.**

When you are hearing about someone else's traumatic event, perhaps on **television**, take the opportunity to **talk** to your child right in that **moment**. Discuss how other people might feel about that experience.

Tell the child how **proud** you are of them when they share a painful feeling with you.

Do not pressure them if they really resist talking to you. This may be a time to consult a therapist.

Use **listening skills** such as, "You feel sad that you were hurt like that."

Be present for the child. He/she may bring up the trauma **when you least expect** it, like in the car or while you are making dinner. Use it as an opportunity to talk.

Coping Strategies

- Provide safety in the home.

- Talk to your child about the trauma.

- Use some drawing techniques.

- Provide therapy for your child and/or yourself.

BONUS: Prenatal experiences can also be traumatic and is a very important part of the birth process. Watch my video to find out how **adoption**, **abandonment** and **parental arguing** affect an unborn child and the **solutions** to help them.

To learn more about these **affects** and get your BONUS CONTENT, please go to this URL:

http://christinealisa.com/WPBook.html

Chapter 5
Dyslexia

Do you know a child who gets exhausted after reading for a short time?

Does your child take long periods of time to finish his/ her homework?

Have you seen children who do not seem to retain what they read?

Does your child have difficulty with spelling and handwriting?

Does your child have trouble following directions?

If you answered yes to these questions, the child may have dyslexia.

As parents we want to help our children in the best ways we can so that they can flourish. Sometimes we run into bumps in the road, but I have found that those obstacles have been lessons for me. I hope you will find the information in this chapter helpful and that you will pass it on to others to improve the future of our children.

What is dyslexia?

Dyslexia is a disorder that interferes with the child's ability to access and process language. In other words, the child struggles with one, two, or all three processes (visual, auditory, and kinesthetic), including imputing material, processing it in the brain, and then outputting it. The areas affected are reading, writing, spelling, handwriting, and sometimes mathematics. There are varying degrees of dyslexia from mild and moderate to severe. It is more common than people think. Some statistics say up to 17 percent of children entering school have some degree of dyslexia, which has nothing to do with intelligence. Rather, it is a neurological problem.

Learning-Related Vision Problems:

A significant percentage of children with dyslexia have it in the form of vision problems. Children may score 20/20 on a school screening test but may have vision problems that go undetected. According to the Optometric Extension Program Foundation, Inc.: "Youngsters must have a variety of scanning, focusing and visual coordination skills for learning and getting meaning from reading. If these visual skills have not been developed, or are poorly developed, learning is difficult and stressful." Vision problems can affect up to 6 percent of children.

Warning Signs of Vision Problems:

When your child is introduced to reading, either in preschool or kindergarten, there will be indicators that your child may have a form of vision-related dyslexia. When the school gives vision tests, none of the signs of dyslexia will be diagnosed. Their tests are mainly for distance and astigmatism issues. These are some of the warning signs of vision problems indicative of dyslexia:

Avoids reading
Holds book very close (seven to eight inches away from eyes).
Occasionally or persistently sees blurring or double vision while reading or writing.
Fatigue and headaches after reading.

Loses place when moving back and forth from looking at a blackboard to his/her page at the child's desk
Writes up or downhill on the page with irregular letter or word spacing.
Blinks excessively and rubs eyes after short periods of reading.
Takes longer to do homework than they should.

Seems to read and understand but then recalls only portions of what he/she read.
Reports that the letters "jump" or "vibrate" on the page
Has a short attention span.

Has difficulty with spelling and handwriting.
Has difficulty learning to tie shoes.
Has trouble memorizing their address, phone number, or the alphabet.

Learning-Related Auditory Problems:

According to KidsHealth.org, another learning difficulty for children is "Auditory Processing Disorder, which affects about 5% of children." They go on to say, "Kids with this condition can't process what they hear in the same way other kids do because their ears and brain don't fully coordinate. Something interferes with the way the brain recognizes and interprets sounds, especially speech."

Learning-Related Auditory Problems Warning Signs:

Your child may have some of these signs and not others, but here are some that indicate a form of dyslexia or auditory problems:

Delayed speech
Chronic ear infections
Stuttering
Trouble following directions
Distracted by background noises
Trouble speaking and expressing him/herself

How the Child Feels and Behaves:

Children with the processing problems of dyslexia feel very frustrated when demands are put on them to read. At school they are expected to follow along with the class. When they cannot keep up with others, their self-esteem is negatively affected. Often they have behavior problems commonly associated with ADHD because they have difficulty focusing. They tend to "space out" to help relieve the tension and fatigue they feel when they cannot achieve the reading skills. If they are diagnosed and treated late (after age seven or eight years), they can feel that there is something wrong with them and end up taking out their anger and frustration on others. If they are diagnosed and enter special education programs in the school setting, they often feel labeled as "different," which can also affect their self-concept.

Dyslexia with Attention Deficit Disorder with Hyperactivity

Oftentimes children with dyslexia also have some form of attention deficit disorder. As a therapist I wonder what came first, dyslexia or attention deficit disorder? Or did ADD/ADHD evolve because of the child's difficulties with language and reading acclimation? A child who struggles with reading becomes distracted and wants to move around or cause a distraction, which looks like ADD/ADHD.

Reading Readiness

Children are not always ready to read when they enter kindergarten, but our schools are pushing early reading. It does not necessarily mean that a child has a learning disability if he/she is not ready to read. Many European schools have known this fact for many years, but here in America we tend to push our children too soon. The usual cutoff for beginning to learn to read is seven years old. There is a tendency for boys to learn to read later than girls, but not always. It has nothing to do with intelligence; it's just a developmental stage characteristic.

Different Learning Styles:

Children have different learning styles. Some are visual learners. Others are auditory learners, and the rest are kinesthetic learners. Children can have strength in one style, but function with the other styles as well. Most of their school life is based on visual and auditory learning skills. However, if your child is predominately kinesthetic, he/she will struggle and develop characteristics that look like ADHD. Kinesthetic learners are those that learn by doing, by touching, by feeling. They are the hands-on learners, the artists, the future carpenters, engineers, and mechanics.

When I was a teacher of fifth graders, I noticed these differences and tried to teach to include these kinesthetic learners. What I discovered amazed me. When I provided woodworking activities, the room was quiet and focused—no disruptions. When I brought out the clay, I discovered students that excelled with their hands creating beautiful pieces of art.

Children's Coping Strategies and How They Best Learn:

Children with dyslexia soon develop coping strategies. They may be high achievers who work extra hard to learn and finish their schoolwork. Their parents spend hours with them at home just trying to finish homework. When I worked as a counselor for the Adult Learning Disability Program at California State University, Long Beach, I saw how hard those students worked to achieve what was so much easier for most everyone else. They had mastered coping skills by working longer and harder. However, the psychological effects of constantly having to cope with the dyslexia created intense anxiety and fear of failure in those students. What impressed me was how these students were determined to not let dyslexia get in the way of their goals. It was a testament to what perseverance can overcome.

Parents: Be Proactive!

If you recognize some of these signs in your child, take action. The younger the child is diagnosed, the better. Seek professionals and trained specialists who diagnose and work with dyslexia. This may entail speaking with your doctor and asking for a referral to a specialist. It may also mean speaking with educational psychologists who test children for learning disabilities. Your child may need to attend sessions with this specialist or another that has been recommended. It may also mean that you will be given specific exercises to do at home with your child.

If your child has visual perceptual difficulties, seek out a doctor that conducts vision therapy. If you child has auditory problems, look for a specialist who works with auditory processing disorder.

The schools do have programs to help your child with learning disabilities. Meet with that school specialist and ask for help to work with your child at home. Maintain a good relationship with that teacher and help your child at home with homework. The more you "partner" with the teachers, the better your child will do at school. Schools do their best, but outside tutoring could also be helpful.

Successful Adults Who Have Dyslexia:

Just to keep you positive, here is a list of some famous people with dyslexia: Albert Einstein, Whoopi Goldberg, Steven Spielberg, Richard Branson, Cher, and Anderson Cooper—just to name a few.

Case Study

Alexis was a fun-loving, sensitive nine-year-old who came from a loving family when she entered therapy. However, she was having trouble sitting still and paying attention in the classroom. She had some anxieties and tended to hold her feelings inside. Alexis hated reading and struggled with homework at home. She told me that she had trouble reading a paragraph top to bottom. She said the letters would "jump around," or she switched the letters. Her mother said that Alexis' eyes would "glaze over" when she was reading at home.

I recommended that Alexis' mother take her to a specialist eye doctor who conducted vision therapy with children. The doctor did diagnose her with dyslexia with visual perceptual problems. The therapy required exercises that Alexis did in the doctor's office and at home, which they did consistently.

My goal for Alexis was to help her focus in the classroom and to dispel some of her anxieties. Her mother spoke to the teacher and asked if Alexis could be allowed to move about in the classroom. Children have so much trouble with sitting for long periods when they have a form of dyslexia and/or attention deficit disorder. The teacher gave Alexis special duties to take notes to the office and opportunities to move around in the classroom, which was very helpful.

In the course of working with Alexis, we found that she had several fears. She was very sensitive to other people's feelings and didn't like bullies. I helped her with how to talk to a bully, which empowered her and worked through a past life where she had been bullied. One day when a girl try to bully her again, Alexis said to her, "Why is it that you always end up crying after this—you know, after you say something to me?"

The girl answered, "I don't cry. You're the one who cries." Then Alexis responded, "Well, when was the last time that you saw me cry?" The girl kind of fumbled and said, "Well, about a week ago you did. You always cry." Alexis came back with, "When was the time before that I cried?" The girl didn't know what to say and walked off. She had remained calm and felt great that she had gotten the girl to back off without being mean as well.

When I work with children who are very sensitive like Alexis, I am sensitive as well to her boundaries. I only talked about the past lives as stories, stories that were inside her that needed to be told so that she didn't have to hold in any feelings. She uncovered a story (lifetime) about a girl who lost her whole family to "mean guys." The whole family was taken away and killed, including herself. I believe this story was a lifetime during the Holocaust where she witnessed her family being beaten and killed and ultimately she was killed herself. There was a lot of sadness and anger that rose up in Alexis, and we used clay to make figures of the mean guys. She pounded these figures with my rubber mallet as she let herself express her anger at them.

When I have a child tell a story with me, I take the elements of the issues that are bothering them and create a scene or scenario. It is like working with metaphor, something that feels very much like what the child's inner world is like. The stories can be the "drivers" that attach to the child and drive their fears. Once a story can be told, the deeper feelings can emerge. In Alexis' case, her inner world was causing her to be distracted, and she had difficulty focusing.

When we discover stories that are scary and involve a feeling of death, shock takes over, and the child wants to avoid that feeling. Allowing the most difficult of feelings to emerge, the child can verbalize what has been "trapped" inside.

Alexis and I found other lifetimes that related to her issue with reading. One was when she was taken from her family to live in a palace as the queen. She again was dealing with separation from family, but there were regulations as the queen. She wasn't allowed to read. I asked her, "How does the girl feel about not being allowed to read?" Alexis answered, "She feels curious about things. She wants to read but can't. She feels locked in." Alexis is allowed to read today, but has difficulty with reading. We call it a "block" in therapy, something that gets in our way. Another lifetime that related to reading was one where she appeared to have dyslexia. She shared the pain she had then of not being able to understand how to read in an era that probably did not know what dyslexia was, much less how to treat it.

By the time Alexis ended her therapy with me, she was getting mostly A's on her report card. Her scores in reading were very high, and she had finished her vision therapy. Her diagnosis of dyslexia was never diagnosed at school, but with outside help she began to understand what she was learning. She was a determined girl who never wanted anyone to know that she had a problem. She was able to reduce many of her anxieties and levels of distractibility. I diagnosed her as having ADD, mostly the inattentive type, but I believe she gained greater control of those issues through our work together. Alexis was a very gifted girl under the confusion of dyslexia, and her talents flourished for her when she made her decision to leave therapy.

My Daughter's Story

When my daughter was in kindergarten, she started having problems sitting still and paying attention when reading skills were taught. She had good experiences in preschool, and we had never noticed any real problems with her. She didn't like to read, but she loved to have her dad and I read to her. I thought that she was just one of those kids who wasn't ready to read. At a parent-teacher conference I was told that my daughter did not seem to be adjusting to kindergarten and showed signs of ADHD. I thought she was just an energetic, exuberant, highly verbal child, but I felt I needed to do something, but what?

Then one day I was talking to a therapist friend of mine about the frustrations we were having, and she suggested I have my daughter diagnosed by a vision specialist. The school's eye test determined she had 20/20 vision, but nothing else. So I took my daughter for her initial exam with the specialist and was dumbfounded. The doctor said she wanted to give my daughter a more extensive exam after her initial consult that very day, which she did not ordinarily do. There was a lot of concern on the doctor's face. Afterwards, she came back with the results. She said that my daughter had severe vision problems. Her eyes did not work together. She had severe amblyopia, which is more commonly known as "lazy eye." She had all the signs of vision-related dyslexia. I was stunned. It was hard to process this information. My daughter is adopted and I know little about any past physical history in her biological family, but I knew I had to take action.

So at the recommendation of the doctor, we began vision therapy twice a week for two years. I worked with the teachers who helped my daughter by putting her near the chalkboard and giving her outlets for her ADHD behavior. She used glasses for a bit, but by age nine did not need those anymore. The treatment was successful!

However, by fifth grade she did not seem to be achieving in reading, and it was of great concern to me. I found a private school where she ultimately achieved well both in reading and writing.

In the course of my daughter's childhood and adolescence, I found therapists, healers, and shamans to help her. I worked with her birth and some of her past lives as well. Being an adoptive child has its own particular issues, and she had symptoms of anxiety and depression, which needed attention.

Here is the happy ending: She no longer has any of the effects of dyslexia or ADHD! She is doing very well in college now, and her professors give her positive feedback on her excellent writing skills. I am very grateful for all the therapists and teachers who have helped her along the way.

I share this story to encourage parents who have a child with dyslexia to intervene early. Have your child tested and evaluated by or before the age of five and continue to be an advocate for their learning. Your child and you will reap great rewards.

Solutions:

Tips to Help Your Child Cope with Dyslexia:

Have them take **breaks** during studying.

Take turns reading homework/books (i.e., you read a paragraph or page and then they read a paragraph or page).

Keep positive, and tell your child **how proud you are** of him/her of their effort.

Provide **physical activity** to work off their frustration and energy.

Have them stand up and/or **change positions** while they read.

Have them **rest their eyes**. Use an icepack or cold cloth to soothe their eyes and head.

Keep your **expectations** reasonable.

Have them do an **art activity**, such as clay or play dough, for a break.

Have them **spin their pencil** back and forth in their fingers while they read or study.

Before a test or homework session, have your child walk around the block **swinging their arms back and forth**. This gets both sides of the brain working together.

Other Actions You Can Take as a Parent:

Believe in your child and try not to worry. Find the joy in the experience.

Have your child **diagnosed early**—by age five, or as soon as possible.

When schools will not test before age eight, have your child **tested by an outside professional**, such as a specialist eye doctor, an optometrist who does vision therapy, or the Irlen Institute, which uses special lenses in glasses if you suspect a visual problem. Look for practitioners in your area.

No approach works for all children. Find the one that works best for yours.

Do eye **exercises** with your child **consistently** if the optometrist, speech therapist, or other practitioner prescribes them.

Work with the school system to get special help for your child, often called "resource program" or "special education."

Be an **advocate for your child** within the school system. Work with the special education teacher and ask what you can do at home.

If the school does not have services for your child, turn to **outside help** such as a therapist or community resources.

Speak up in the community, social media, or interest groups to bring the issues of dyslexia to the world. **Educate others**.

Quick Win Strategies:

- Look for warning signs of dyslexia and have your child diagnosed.

- Find a program, doctor, or practitioner to help your child.

- Stay positive and support your child.

- Be creative and allow your child to be an individual.

- Be an advocate for your child in the schools.

Chapter 6
Sexual Abuse

Do you know of a child who has all the warning signs of being sexually abused?

Has your child been sexually abused and you are seeking help?

Do you believe that the effects of sexual abuse can be fully healed?

Do you want to know how to talk to a child who has been sexually abused?

When we hear of a child who has been sexually abused, it breaks our hearts. This violation of a child goes so deep and leaves the adults feeling helpless and angry.

Unfortunately, it is more widespread than we think, and I include this chapter to widen all our eyes to this phenomenon in our culture. My goal is for children and their parents to feel more empowered and clear of the effects of sexual abuse.

Warning Signs of Sexual Abuse:

A child who has been sexually abused displays various symptoms and behaviors. The signs differ depending on the age of the child, but the most significant are any sudden changes in behavior, such as shifts in eating habits, shutting down or withdrawal from others, nightmares, and regressed behavior like acting younger than their current age. Physical indicators range from chronic stomachaches to pain or itching in the genital area and chronic yeast infections. Behaviors that were formerly uncharacteristic of the child, such as sexualized behavior, compulsive masturbation, excessively touching the privates of other children, and explicit talk about sex, are indicators of sexual abuse. The child can also be depressed and anxious.

A teenager who has been sexually abused may show excessive signs of sexuality, such as posting nude pictures online and arranging a meeting with an online acquaintance, compulsive masturbation beyond the norm, and sexual harassment of others. Cutting, dressing provocatively, seeking out multiple sexual partners, and obsessive viewing of pornography coupled with depression and anxiety can also be signs.

Basically, anything outside the range of normal behavior that is excessive and has the element of being demeaning or sexually aggressive is a warning sign to pay close attention to as a parent, guardian, or teacher.

Statistics:

According to the studies done by David Finkelhor, director of the Crimes Against Children Research Center, one out of five girls and one out of twenty boys are victims of child sexual abuse. However, the National Center for Victims of Crime states, "Obtaining accurate statistics is difficult because sexual abuse is not often reported."

These statistics are alarming to all of us. It is shocking and overwhelming to think of the number of children who are treated so badly. I personally feel that the numbers are higher than what has been reported because of the nature of sexual abuse and the secrecy attached to it.

According to a study published online and in the *Journal of Adolescent Health,* "Compared to those with no history of sexual abuse, young males who were sexually abused were five times more likely to cause teen pregnancy, three times more likely to have multiple sexual partners and two times more likely to have unprotected sex." Our young people's lives are being so altered by the effects of molestation that it begs the question, what are we doing to stop this crisis? It is such a huge problem that I have chosen to include a chapter to not only help parents feel they are not alone, but to inspire us to do more to heal the children who have suffered from sexual abuse and their families as well. Abuse is my personal global issue.

What to Do if These Signs Occur: Find a Therapist

Finding a therapist who specializes in working with child sexual abuse is the imperative. Along with credentials and experience in child sexual abuse, there are other things to look for in a therapist. Some questions to ask include the following: Does the therapist establish safety and trust with your child? Does the therapist explain the process of therapy to you so that you understand what to expect? Do you and your child relate to the therapist, i.e., how comfortable are you both? Does the therapist offer you parenting skills? Feeling like you have a competent professional to help you and your child navigate the emotional ups and downs in therapy is essential.

Communicating with Your Child:

Once your child has told you that he/she has been molested, there are some guidelines to follow. Believe your child. Try to stay nonreactive. Do not get angry at the alleged perpetrator in front of the child. Stay present and prepare yourself to listen to the child. Be loving and kind. Tell your child that you have to report the abuse to the authorities. It is the law because this person needs to never hurt another child again. If your child objects to you reporting, tell them it is not his/her fault. The perpetrator was wrong, not the child. Perpetrators need to learn that they cannot do those things to children. Keep the lines of communication open with your child by listening nonjudgmentally, respecting their privacy, and creating a safe environment.

The Stages Children Go through in Therapy:

Once the child enters therapy with me, they go through various stages.

Stage #1: Creating Safety

Children are looking to see if they are safe to tell me things and I will believe them. I always believe the child. Children "test" to see if I will allow certain kinds of behavior in the therapy session, so I set limits—what I will allow and what I won't. Children who have been abused need limits to help them feel safe because their sense of safety was jeopardized. This is a time when the child may not want to talk about the abuse to the parent. Children who have had to talk to the authorities can be re-traumatized and may refuse to talk about it. I allow children space to talk when they are ready.

During this period of therapy, it is very common for children to "recant" what they disclosed originally. Younger children especially seem to change or deny the abuse. This is typical. Children's minds are different from adults, and they can feel pressured from other adults to keep quiet. I have had children in therapy whose relatives have threatened them and told them not to talk about what happened. My job is to build the sense of self of the child strong enough that they can trust themselves and the protective parent or safe adults.

I advise the parent/guardian to establish safety in the home. If the abuser is a family member who is not in jail but living in the home, keeping the child safe is more difficult. If the abuser has been ordered to receive therapy and lives in the home, it is then the responsibility of the non-offending parent to keep that child safe and the offending parent to not threaten or abuse the child in any way.

Stage #2: Dealing with Feelings

My goal as a therapist is to re-empower children whose sense of self has been reduced or who suffer from low self-esteem. I provide experiences for the children to express their anger, fear, helplessness, confusion, and sadness. This is a stage where the parent can initiate release of feelings at home by having the child hit a pillow, scream into a pillow, use a plastic bat to hit a pillow, or draw a picture and tear it, up among other techniques.

As children express more feelings, they may regress. That means that they might have "accidents" more often and seem to have lost their potty-training accomplishments. They may be clingy and want to be treated like a baby. A teenager will seem to be acting much younger than his/her age. There may be incidents of wetting the bed, trouble with concentrating in school, isolation, or trouble with peers. This is a stage when it looks to the parent like things are getting worse before they get better, but that is to be expected.

Stage #3: More Involvement of the Family

Having the child or teenager speak to the family about their experience in a safe, therapeutic session when the child is ready is an important part of the healing process. I personally believe that when the child is ready to talk— and not before—the therapy will be successful. There will be moments of fear of facing the truth and/or the perpetrator, but my goal is to strengthen the inner world of the child and to help the child be free of the effects of being abused.

Through all these stages I involve the parent or guardian by explaining certain behaviors and symptoms and giving suggestions of what to do at home.

Coping as the Non-Offending Parent

If the sexual abuse has occurred within the family unit, the non-offending parent is left to deal with the "aftermath" of the secret being revealed. It can be a shattering time in a parent's life. Everything seems like it is crumbling down; all the safety nets seem to have been removed. It is natural for the non-offending parent to go through a period of denial, disbelief, anger, sadness, and grief. Finding networks of support is very helpful at this time. Being kind to oneself without self-criticism can be a struggle as the parent tries to find some sense in the behaviors of the perpetrator that make no sense at all. Reaching out to safe, loving family members and friends is essential for this parent. Learning to lean on others and finding a good therapist who specializes in working with parents of abused children are both very important.

When I work with the non-offending parent in therapy, issues come up around divorce, custody, lawyers, the justice system, police, social workers, and health-care providers. Disclosure of abuse is a crisis, and parents need help maneuvering through it.

Dealing with the challenges of the "system" of social workers and police and a judicial system made up of public defenders, district attorneys, lawyers, and judges is often intimidating for parents and the child. Many of these people are doing the best that they can to protect children. However, in their attempt to prosecute the offender or protect the child, there are often roadblocks. Many courts now are appointing children their own attorney, which is a good sign. Such was the situation in the following case.

Case Study

I had a case of a quiet, bright, high-achieving eleven-year-old girl I call Katie, who had been molested by a close family friend who was like a father to her. Her mother was a single mom who trusted the family friend to provide a male role model for her daughter. On the day the daughter told her mother, she reported it to the authorities. Two members of the police department arrived at the home, a man and a woman. They required Katie to speak to them separately from their mother, which is typical. However, they asked her to repeat the story over and over, trying to get more details because they wanted the perpetrator to go to jail. This added pressure was difficult for Katie because she didn't like talking to strangers about any personal matters. She ended up being traumatized again by these overzealous officers who did not understand the ramifications of their pressure on a young girl.

After a period of time of speaking with social workers and the deputy district attorney, Katie's mother was able to get Katie her own attorney. She also entered therapy with me, and we began doing the healing work together. My first goal with Katie was to help her give voice to her anger at the officials in the system and to establish a safe place to do that. She was unwilling to talk about the molestation for some time, and I respected that. However, Katie could also talk about the anger she had at other people, kids at school, and homework. I used clay to pound, drawings to rip up and bash to pieces, and puppets to dialog with to strengthen her. I gave Katie a sense of control by playing silly games with her, giving her choices in the session, and being an adult that did not expect anything of her.

We did a lot of role-playing exercises where she practiced speaking to the judge. By the time she had to appear in court, Katie was fully ready to stand her ground in front of the perpetrator. Her strength was building, and she began to speak about her sadness and loss around not having the family friend in her life anymore. Children experience a profound betrayal that is hard for them to express. Eventually, with my guidance she was able to go deeply into the pain and tell me what he had done. She released her emotional connection to him and the false belief that it was her job to take care of him, which he had manipulated her to do. At the close of therapy, her mother told me she had her daughter back. There was a skip in her step and a smile on her face. She was making more friends and feeling less pressured in her life. She wasn't taking her performance at school as compulsively as she had and was welcoming new experiences with glee.

Strategies for Working with the System

I have worked with an excellent program in one county in Southern California where I practiced that had one site where the child and parent were taken. While a social worker interviewed the child, the police were on the other side of the two-way mirror. If there was penetration, a specialist doctor or nurse was available to examine the child. Everything was done one time on-site. If you have a program in your area like that, I would suggest you take your child to that facility. Some police officers are trained to interview children and social workers as well.

Work with the social workers and police, but also speak up for your child.

Get advice from an attorney on your rights and your child's rights.

Take and keep notes. When your child tells you something important, write it down. If your child shows any signs of sexual abuse, write it down. You may need those notes later.

Check to see if there are any court advocates who could help you.

Family Dynamics

In my experience there are some similarities and differences in the family dynamics of sexual abuse within the family and outside the family. If it is abuse outside the family, there is a range of feelings toward that perpetrator and each other. I worked with a family whose three-year-old boy had been molested by stranger in a restroom of a child-oriented restaurant. Each member of the family had feelings of guilt, blame, helplessness, confusion, anger, and a sense of victimization until they worked it out individually and together in therapy.

In families where the perpetrator is a family member, many of the same feelings occur, but there are huge disruptions in the family. Families who experience sexual abuse have a system of secrecy and denial. When the secret is out, some members will turn on each other and/or blame the other. Families become divided. I have worked with families where the perpetrator verbally attacked the non-offending parent and cohered the child victim into believing what he is doing is their "special game." He tried to convince the child that what they were doing (sexual games) wasn't wrong. This caused the child to become confused and divided and to doubt herself.

The issue of codependency is clearly manifested in the family system where sexual abuse exists. Family members may "know" at some level that the abuse is going on, but they protect themselves through denial to avoid a crisis if the truth is revealed. Some non-offending parents were actually victims of sexual abuse themselves and need to pursue their own therapy to resolve those issues. In doing so, they become healthier and better parents. I always tell parents, "The better you are, the better your child will be."

Solutions

Improve Your Communication with the Child or Teenager

Parents can support the child by taking time to reassure the child, listen to his/her feelings, and try to understand the **child's point of view** by:

Speaking gently and **nonjudgmentally** to your child or teen

Avoiding blaming, arguing, giving advice, or lecturing

Owning your own feelings whenever possible or appropriate, e.g., "I am very saddened by what has happened to you."

Listen to their feelings and **reflect** them back to them, e.g., "You are very hurt by what _____ did and you wish it could just all go away."

Telling them **they are safe now** and you are doing your best to make that true for them.

Being **honest** about your part and **apologize** for anything you did that you regret. Expect that your child/ teen will be angry and will lash out at times. Remember to give them **safe outlets** for that anger.

Being **respectful** of your child's/teen's feelings. If they want a therapist where everything is confidential, hold to that.

Have an Action Plan

Find a therapist or healer for your child/teen and your own therapist to explore your own **codependency issues**.

If alcohol or drug abuse is involved, join a **twelve-step program** and build your life back.

If there are **groups** for children/teens in your area for **sexual abuse**, interview the leaders to determine if it would be helpful.

If you are stimulated **or triggered** into your own childhood issues, explore them with a therapist and/or a support group.

Work to develop **trust** in yourself and build trust between you and your child/teen. If you say you are going to do something, **keep your word**.

Find **outlets for your feelings**. e.g., talking with close friends, screaming in the car with the windows closed while parked in a safe area, doing stress-release exercises such as Emotional Freedom Technique, breathing and writing in a journal.

Take a **self-defense** class. Offer your child the opportunity to take a self-defense class.

If appropriate, **consult an attorney**.

Recap of the Solution for Quick Action:

- Open your communication with your child/teen.

- Find a qualified therapist for your child/teen and yourself.

- Seek support from others.

- Explore outlets for releasing feelings that work best for you and your child.

- Work on yourself to rebuild trust.

Chapter 7
Physical Abuse

Have you seen suspicious bruising or marks on your child's body?

Do you know a teenager that wears long-sleeve shirts and pants regularly, even on a hot day?

Are you worried about a teenager you know that seems excessively sullen and noncommunicative?

Does your child exhibit a "startle" response to experiences and cringe around adults?

Warning Signs of Physical Abuse

Children who have been physically abused have both physical indicators and behavioral symptoms to be aware of when determining if they have been physically abused.

They may have frequent injuries that are unexplained or in areas where children do not usually injure themselves, such as the back, neck, thighs, or buttocks. Welts or bruising that seem to show in clusters or cigarette burns are clear signs of abuse. If a child wears inappropriate clothing, such as long pants and shirts on a hot day, there is a high probability that the child has been abused; the necessity for an adult to check those areas is essential.

Warning signs show up differently depending on the child's developmental stage (age range.) The young child will cringe often, have frequent startle responses such as flinching when touched, have poor attention span, be confused under pressure, and be fearful and on high alert. They can also be sneaky. A child who is a little older will be aggressive (often in boys) or withdrawn (often in girls). Lying, poor self-esteem, and difficulty concentrating takes place in this six- to twelve-year-old range. Teenagers will be sullen and excessively resistant to communicating with others. They may show little interest in school and may be manipulative and defensive. They are very vulnerable to substance abuse at this age.

Statistics

According to www.childhelp.org, "A child abuse report is made every ten seconds in the United States. Every year 3 million reports of child abuse are made involving more than 6 million children." A CDC/Kaiser Permanente Adverse Childhood Experiences Study found that "physical abuse had the highest percentage of cases: 28.3%. In 2012 state agencies estimated that 1,640 children died as a result of abuse and neglect. That is between four and five a day." According to the National

Children's Alliance, "18% of the children suffered physical abuse."

These statistics leave us with a great hole of pain inside. That children can be so maltreated with little regard for the enormity of the problem is a travesty. My global challenge is to awaken us and bring hope to the parents whose children suffer from abuse, which is a blow to all humanity. Abuse creates a crisis of meaning in our lives. We all have a responsibility to our fellow man/child, do we not?

What to Do if These Signs Occur

First of all, report the abuse. A social worker from the department of social services will call you, ask for more information, and come out to the home to talk to the child and alleged abuser. If the police are called, they will come out and interview as well. Then find a therapist who specializes in child abuse. There are therapists in private practice who are highly qualified, but there are also agencies and clinics that have in-house therapists who specialize with abuse.

Strategies to Work with the "System"

There are many possible outcomes that will happen once the report is made. They range from court-ordered therapy for the child and for the offending parent and non-offending parent, to incarceration of the offending parent and removal of the child from the home, to no follow-up at all. However, if a social worker has been assigned to the case, it is very important that the parents consistently follow the guidelines presented to them. Sometimes the court will order anger-management and parenting classes. If a non-offending parent or relative makes repeated reports to the department of social services with very little to no response from that agency, continue to make those reports anyway. Then everything is documented.

Case Studies

I want to share two cases of children in the same family that I worked with for a time. These two girls, Becky and Emily, were two of four children who were neglected and physically abused by their father and mother. Their grandmother had tried to intercede at times but was unsuccessful until a report of abuse was made and she became their guardian.

After the grandmother selected me as the children's therapist, she and I worked together brainstorming strategies to be advocates for the children. We worked together to face the challenges that came from social services and the school system. During the course of therapy, the parents lost custody of the girls, and the grandmother adopted them. This family is very close to my heart. I was a witness to the strength of individuals both young and older going through the healing process and coming out the other side with renewed hope. It is with joy that I share their story.

Emily was six years old when she started sessions with me. Her father had abused her physically and both parents were neglectful. She often did not get enough to eat. As is often common in families of abuse, Emily took on the role of the protector. She would tell me how she had put herself in her father's way so that he would hit her instead of the other siblings. It was her way of making sure in her own mind that the others would not be hurt. She also had kept many of her memories of the abuse and was the spokesperson for her siblings to continually remind them not to forget what both parents did to them.

She was an angry child, often hitting, pinching, and pushing kids at school and being defiant with adults. Her anger was her defense mechanism. She told me that her dad would come back in her mind at school and she would act out her anger at others. As long as she was oppositional, she could feel some sense of control in her life. However, it became clear that she was identifying with the aggressor. In other words, Dad was the one who had the most power in the family, so Emily took on those characteristics to avoid being the victim. We spent time using anger techniques to release all the stored-up anger. She described seeing pictures of monsters on her ceiling at night. Those monsters were of her dad. We drew pictures of Dad, yelled at him, shot darts at the pictures of him, and pounded clay figures of him. Emily and her siblings would often wake up in the middle of the night and play together. It was a way to stay vigilant and safe. Abused children do not feel safe. Emily would talk about seeing her dad beat her mom, and there was nothing she could do about it.

One day I brought up something that her grandma had told me. She said that Emily's father would throw Emily against the wall. I recreated the incident using props and clay in my child therapy room and asked her what he was saying when he threw her against the wall. She said he called her a bad name and told her to get out of his way. Emily proceeded to slump down and shut down. This is what we call emotional shock. It is the body's reaction to trauma. I asked her to breathe with me and move through it. As she stared into space, she breathed with me, breathing out shock. The staring into space is called dissociation, which means to detach from association, i.e., to not be present.

Then she put her hands around her neck and slumped down on the floor, telling me that he had his hands on her throat. Saying her father's words aloud and hearing me repeat them stimulated the experience of being choked and the accompanying shock. Once she put her own hands around her neck, I knew that she was recreating what her dad had done to her. I help her reframe the experience by telling her that he was gone, that she was safe now, and it was all over while I rocked her like a baby. It is important for children reliving these experiences to have them reframed so that they can ground themselves into current reality and put a boundary on the experience.

In a subsequent session she was able to go deeper into the choking experience and told me she was afraid that she was going to die. In the course of working with any abused child, the therapist must find the place where the child thought she died. By working together with the child and validating that she did not die, I can enable her to begin to release that fear. These sessions were a breakthrough for Emily. She had released a critical piece of the abuse she had suffered at the hands of her father.

Here is the happy ending. After working with me for a while, Emily stopped her aggressive behavior, finished her schoolwork on time, got good grades, talked easily and respectfully to other adults, and stopped her protective behavior.

Her sister, Becky, was four years old when she first came to see me. She had nightmares of monsters and had difficulty going to sleep at night. She had been potty-trained but was now experiencing encopresis, which means she would hold her bowels for a while until she would go in her underwear.

During her sessions, she would repeatedly paint splotches of red and black on the paper. She wouldn't tell me anything about them for several sessions until one day she said the red was blood and the black was her mom. I drew a picture of a boy with a scared face since I introduce feeling words to small children. She drew red over him, which she said was blood and her dad had killed him. Then she said her dad killed her sister. I know these words are not clear as yet, but I do not question them.

The following session she came in determined to tell me something. She started to paint red and black again. I asked her to tell me about it, and she said, "It is blood. There is a knife and a lady getting cut. A bad man is killing her with the knife." I asked, "Where is the lady getting cut?" She pointed to her own chest, and I asked, "When the man cuts her with the knife, what happens to her?" She answered, "There is blood." I asked, "What happens when there is blood, just the first thing that pops in your mind?" Becky answered, "She's killed." I told her, "We know that it is over now. When she dies, the bad man is gone." We breathed together and she felt better. This session was a past life that she experienced. I am not here to prove that there are past lives, but Dr. Ian Stevenson and Dr. Jim Tucker have documented young children spontaneously speaking of their past lives.

89

When I ask for a history from the parents or guardians before I begin therapy with a child, I include in my questionnaire one about birth. Becky's grandmother indicated that Becky had been born in the bathroom. After the birth her great-uncle called for the ambulance, and she and her mother soon went to the hospital.

In her subsequent sessions she told me about her birth after painting more red and black. She said that the black was her mother and the red was blood. She went on to say that her mother was screaming and scared. She was in the bathroom, and there was blood over her mom and that this was Becky being born. She said that the ambulance came and they went to the hospital when the umbilical cord was cut. She was breathing on her own, and it was over; the trauma was over. I asked her what the scariest part of that birth was for her, and she said, "My mom was going to die, and I was going to die." She also said that she didn't want to go back to her mom's tummy because her dad was mean and hit her mom.

It is not uncommon to find domestic violence in families where there is abuse. Usually the mother is the victim, and the father is the abuser, but not always. Children are also victimized when they witness their mother being abused because they feel helpless and at risk.

Since I do alternative therapy with children, I include these past unconscious places where trauma has been recorded in the body and mind. These are often the stuck, scary places that need to be talked about and released by the child. Becky's therapy finally crystallized one day when she was able to relive a terrifying event when her father was terrorizing the rest of the family, grabbing Becky from where she was hiding under a table and driving away with her in the car, threatening to never bring her back. She had been holding this event in her body by tensing and not releasing her bowels.

The good news to Becky's story is that not only did the encopresis stop, but she also learned how to stand up to kids at school who tried to make fun of her. She was now at ease in her body, safe at home, and free to speak her mind.

Helping the Parent Understand the Process of Therapy

There is a process, and I explain to the parents what they might expect. Children will need your support and understanding in several ways. They may be overwhelmed with feelings, throw tantrums, hit a sibling, or destroy something in the house. Clearly state your limit in those areas and talk to them. Listen to what they say because the trauma is being re-enacted. This is a time to be there for the child and not yell, blame, overly punish, or lecture. It may seem like they are getting worse, not better when these incidents occur, but it really means the therapy is working.

Children may regress, or act younger than their age. This is normal because the abuse may have started at an earlier time in their life. The parent needs to stay calm, not be critical, and comfort the child. I have had children who want their parent to cuddle with them and pretend they are babies again. This is nourishing for the child and does not mean that they will stay that way.

Family therapy helps the parent and child to find new ways to have fun together and reestablish their bond, and it gives them tools to better communicate. I believe that it is essential that the child not be asked to go into family therapy with the abuser if the child is still afraid of that parent. As the child's sense of self strengthens and the abuser has worked individually to clear his abusive behavior, family therapy can be a very healing experience.

Solutions:

Things a Non-Offending Parent/Guardian Can Do at Home if the Abuser Has Been Removed from the Home:

Reassure children that they are safe. Check locked windows, under the bed, and in the closet with young children. Have **people in your life** who are safe.

Give them **outlets** for their feelings. Get them a plastic **whiffle bat** and a pillow to hit when they are **angry**. Sit with them and help them get angry as they hit the pillow.

Read books to them that help support the **scary feelings** and talk about how scary it was.

Draw pictures of what happened and **tear** them up. Tear up old magazines and throw them in the trash.

If the child has to see the abuser through **court-ordered monitored visits**, listen to their feelings. Often these visits can set off an emotional setback. See if a **court ordered advocate** could be there to give additional support.

If the Abuser Is Not a Family Member

If someone **outside the family** has physically abused the child, it could be a family friend, teacher, trusted authority figure, or a stranger. All of these are traumatic experiences. These abuse situations affect the **whole family** and put them in **crisis.** Each family member will react emotionally and will need **guidance** to best maneuver the **law enforcement** and judicial issues as well as the feelings of being victimized. The family as a whole and as individuals feels **helpless** and **angry.**

I have worked with families where the child had to appear in court because of abuse by a trusted teacher. Unfortunately, these cases we see are more prevalent in our news each day. This crisis of violence in our society is invading our sense of safety and predictability and is giving us a sense of loss of control. I advise that all family members **reach out for support and therapy**, find **groups** that are **taking action against abusers**, and join us in stopping this epidemic. No one can take our power away unless we let them.

Coping Strategies for the Non-Offending Parent if the Physical Abuser Is Still in the Home:

Put together a **treatment program for yourself** that might include individual therapy, group therapy, codependent classes, and parenting classes.

Do not stay isolated. Utilize the support of **healthy** family members or friends or find a support group.

Get stronger emotionally, mentally, and physically by **working on yourself**. You will be a **role model** for your children, showing them how not to be abused in the future.

Utilize **family therapy** and couples therapy to change the **communication** patterns.

If the offending parent is not willing to make any changes for the positive, you may need to separate. See a lawyer for a consultation.

Empowering the Non-Abuser

Very often the parent who does not physically harm the child is a victim of domestic violence. The parent often has to flee the home and go to a domestic violence safe house where she can receive therapy and practical help in rebuilding his/her life.

There are also groups for **victims of domestic violence**. Look for a **program** in your community or a hotline.

Check out if there are Victims of Crime **programs** in your community. There maybe **other resources** for the family like safe houses for domestic violence victims.

Take a self-defense class. Very often the non-offending parent was a victim of child abuse and needs to do a physical remapping to **change the victimization pattern.**

Enter therapy and **explore the patterns** that caused you to become involved in a relationship with an abuser.

Reach out to groups who are raising consciousness about abuse and **taking action** to stop the offenders.

Recap of the Solution for Quick Action

- Keep the children safe and report abuse.

- Reach out in the community for services.

- Place the child in therapy.

- Enter personal therapy.

- Empower yourself through community action.

Chapter 8
Mental Abuse

Do you have a child who is very critical of herself?

Does your child have poor self-esteem?

Does your child hold things inside that you know are bothering him?

Do you know a child who is clingy with people she doesn't know that well?

What is mental abuse?

Mental abuse is also termed "emotional abuse." These terms can be used interchangeably. According to the National Society for the Prevention of Cruelty to Children, "Emotional abuse is the ongoing emotional maltreatment or emotional neglect of a child. It is sometimes called psychological abuse and can seriously damage a child's emotional health and development."

There are many forms of mental abuse that a child experiences from a parent or guardian. Negative verbal criticisms, threats, and put-downs are common characteristics of mental abuse. The adult constantly blaming or shaming the child constitutes emotional abuse. Behaviors from the parent or guardian of a passive-aggressive nature confuse the child and make them believe that there is something wrong with them, e.g., promising to do something for the child and then turning around and not doing it.

When children hear negative talk directed at them, they begin to believe those words because they have no defenses against them. Children have not developed defense mechanisms like adults. Teachers and therapists can report emotional abuse to social services, but it is hard to prove since there are no telltale marks or allegations of sexual violation. However, it still affects children and their sense of self. As a therapist I report emotional abuse even if social services does not take action or find proof. Social workers usually have to make a written report, and those reports remain on file, creating a history.

Symptoms of Mental Abuse:

Children who have suffered from mental abuse can show various symptoms such as poor self-esteem, a drop in grades or consistently doing poor schoolwork, shutting down internally, being very quiet or shy, lacking friends, or having poor social skills. They may be very critical of themselves and get frustrated easily when doing their schoolwork. They may act out by calling names or bullying other students. They can also be the objects of a bully because they are familiar with being bullied at home. They may have a hard time controlling their strong emotions and are clingy or overly affectionate with people they do not know very well.

Children Who Are Emotionally Abused Are Often the Victims of Other Types of Abuse or Neglect

Through my years of experience, I have seen children who have undergone mental/emotional abuse. However, in many cases those children also have experienced some other type of abuse. It is not uncommon for children who have been emotionally abused to have also been physically or sexually abused or even victims of neglect.

If parents have endured abuse themselves as children, they are more likely to use some sort of abuse on their own child. When parents get "stimulated" into reactions coming from their own childhood, they have an unconscious reaction to their own children. They take on the parenting practices of their own parents. However, there are parents who reframe from the physical abuse and primarily abuse their child emotionally. When I work with families, I try to work with each parent individually to help them uncover their own childhood issues. I have found over the years that adults can choose positive parenting strategies after they have cleared the effects of their own childhood.

It is such a sad thing when abuse takes form in a family. So many people do not get proper guidance on how to truly take care of their children. In my therapy practice I educate families on different ways they can raise their children through love, understanding, communication, healthy limit setting, and healing the unconscious pain in each of them.

Case Study

Jason was nine years old when his father brought him to therapy with me. Jason was a boy who had experienced verbal and emotional abuse as well as physical abuse. After his parent's divorce he had been living with his mother in another state. His father, who had just gone through cancer treatments, worked to get custody of Jason after two incidents that happened in the classroom. One day, after Jason's special education teacher put him in time-out for throwing papers around the room, he crunched himself in a corner and cried. He told her, "I don't want to live anymore. I want to die. I can't do anything right." Then another day that week Jason tried to choke himself. The teacher stopped him and sent him to the school psychologist. His mother was told to provide outside therapy for Jason, but she did not follow through. His final incident in the classroom was banging his head against the wall, kicking, screaming, and throwing himself around. It was at that point that he went to live with his father and stepmother.

When Jason came to me, he could not concentrate in school or even finish a test. He was intelligent, but below grade level. He was put into a resource program, which is special education. One day on the playground, Jason fell off the jungle gym and had to be taken to the emergency room. He had broken his arm and was screaming, "I'm going to die." He couldn't calm down, and when the doctor and nurse tried to hold him down, he screamed and kicked them.

I had him make a sand-tray scene of what happened on the jungle gym. It was clear that the trauma of breaking his arm had unleashed the trauma of his earlier childhood. He told me that his mother used to say bad things to him when she hit him with a belt. She would also punish him when his sister had done something wrong and blamed him. He felt like his mother didn't love him. In our sessions we did a lot of anger work because he was holding a lot of rage inside him. He had even taken a kitchen knife and hit the cutting board over and over. In a family session with his stepmother, dad, and sister, we started a line of communication to bring the secrets that Jason had been carrying into the open.

When I work with children who have been emotionally abused, one of my goals is to find any negative words that the parent said to the child. These words are often what I call the "glue" that keeps the child caught in the effects of abuse. If we can find the words and externalize those words, the child can remember more of what happened to him and release his rage in a safe environment with no judgment. Some of the things his mother had said included calling him names (e.g., the "F" word, *stupid*, and *dumb*) and telling him that he never tried in school and that he would never see his father again, which he said, "felt like a needle piercing my heart." His father could have died from cancer, so the fear was intense.

Emotional abuse can also appear in the birth process. How the mother feels about having a child is recorded in the child's unconscious mind. I explained to Jason that he had a deeper mind that acted much like a tape recorder. It stored the words, feelings, and physical experience of a baby coming into the world. Jason's birth was Cesarean, but before his mother was given drugs, she was thinking about having the baby. She did not want the baby, and she did not want a boy. She was very angry, and her thoughts mirrored that anger: "I'm going to get even with this baby. This little baby is going to get it when he's older. I'm going to treat him like dirt." She wanted to give him up for adoption. When he was removed through Cesarean, he wasn't breathing, and the doctor said, "We're losing him." They had to put him in an incubator for a couple weeks. He also heard words spoken by both his parents regarding whether they were going to keep him or give him up for adoption. His father wanted him, but his mother did not. These words and attitudes of his parents created issues of abandonment and hopelessness in Jason that were connected unconsciously to his survival pattern: coming alive meant not being wanted and fear of maltreatment.

Jason's mother used verbal threats along with spanking and locking him in his room when his father was not around, leaving him feeling isolated and hopeless. In his current life he was active in sports; however, he was erratic in his performance. Sometimes he would do well, and then it was as if he lost the use of his legs. He gave up. He would slow down or quit altogether, leaving his team in the lurch. His father was his coach and would accuse his son of "wimping out." This verbal put-down only made it worse, so I started working with his father individually in therapy to help him understand himself and Jason.

A breakthrough happened one day in therapy when Jason found the scariest incident of his young childhood. By accessing the hopelessness coming from his unconscious mind, he found a scene where his mother had a knife in one hand and was choking Jason with her other hand.

When he couldn't breathe and was afraid he was going to die, she said, "I am going to cut your legs off with the knife. You better not ever tell your dad or you will get it." The source of his pattern of giving up was the feeling that he was going to die and that there was nothing he or anyone could do about it. I explained to him that this was what we therapists call a double bind, which means no matter what he did, something bad would happen. If he told his dad, his fear was that his mother would kill him.

When children have such a profound experience of feeling like they are going to die, such as Jason had, I make sure that we clear any past life that may be keeping him in that fear. He also was told that he could not tell his father about his mother's threats, which he did for fear of his own life. So we found a lifetime where Jason had been a prisoner of war in Vietnam. He had been captured at knifepoint, wounded, and tortured. His torturers cut off his legs, but he never gave the enemy any information that would harm his fellow soldiers. A knife was used in three ways in Jason's past: one was his birth, the use of a knife for the Cesarean; the second was his mother using the knife at his face when she was choking him; and the third was the past life when he was led by knifepoint and ultimately killed by cutting off his legs.

Jason believed that he would never have any protection from his mother, so we worked on getting his power back and eliminating that false belief. We all develop beliefs from our childhood, and Jason was no exception. He kept reenacting the hopelessness until one day he told me that he changed that belief. His mother came for a visit after Jason had not seen her in a long time. He stood firm and clear in his mother's presence and was able to score a goal in his sport while she watched.

At his graduation session he told me something that I will never forget. He said, "I beat the bogeyman!" He was getting mostly A's in his classes at school and was no longer in the special education program. He was elected president of his sixth-grade student council, had many friends, and was confident in his sport. He stood up for himself now and was nobody's victim anymore.

Other Situations Where Emotional Abuse Takes Place:

I have seen children in therapy who have been mentally/emotionally abused, but who have not suffered any other abuse. In some of those cases, the parents find it hard to show love to the child, and the child does not feel good about herself. In other cases the child and the parent clash for many reasons. For example, the child is very different from the parent, and so the parent finds it hard to relate to that child. This leaves the parent frustrated and the child believing that there is something wrong with him/her. It is no one's fault, but it is the job of the therapist to find a "bridge" from the parent to the child. We can find that bridge in family therapy where each person is able to express their feelings and start to look at new ways to accept each other.

When working with past-life therapy in a family, we find that family members have been together before in other lifetimes. By doing the deep conscious work to understand why they are together again, those bridges can be built. I have seen so many beautiful revelations occur where parents discover their deeper connection to their child.

If children are neglected emotionally and their basic needs are not met consistently, they are mentally/ emotionally abused. Their sense of safety and well-being is at risk. Children who live in homes where there is little contact between parent and child or where the child feels the need to become the parent suffer. Some parents have had emotionally deprived lives as children, and they are just imitating the patterning of their youth.

Emotional Effects of Divorce on Children

Though parents are not choosing to mentally abuse their child when they obtain a divorce, the children do suffer emotionally. Their lives are disrupted, and they often travel back and forth between households. In my experience children are afraid to talk to one or both parents about how they feel because they do not want to lose the love of either parent. They do not want one parent to tell the other parent how they feel, so they stuff it inside, or they feel a need to protect a parent who has been hurt by the divorce. Ultimately, they want their parents to get back together and feel sad when this never happens. They have lost some of their stability and need to regain it back again.

In divorce cases I have been a witness to one parent being the "dominant" parent and the other taking less responsibility for the child. One parent is the active parent, and the other takes little interest in the child's life. Or one parent puts down the other parent in front of the child. These imbalances can create confusion in the child. When children gets confused, they tend to fill in the blanks. /They think it is their fault because there can be no other answer. It is the way a children's minds work.

Solutions:

Communication Suggestions for Parents

Change your language with your child. **Avoid** put-downs, criticisms, or threats. They do not bring about the results you would like, only negative reactions.

Own your feelings. If you are frustrated with your child, say that, e.g., "I am frustrated." Find ways to **release your feelings** like writing in a journal or talking to a friend.

Notice if your **buttons are being pushed**. Is your child stimulating some memory from your childhood that has gone unresolved?

Are you getting overly angry? Take out your anger elsewhere, not at your child. Doing something physically safe before you try to talk to your child actually **gives you more control.**

Find **neutral places** to talk to your child, and encourage them to tell you how they felt about something you said or did. **Listen** without reacting.

Listen to your child even **if you do not agree** with them. Model a positive behavior that your child will imitate. The more you listen, the more apt the child is **willing** to listen and **talk** to you.

If you have said something you regret, **apologize** to your child and try not to say it again.

Especially in a situation of **divorce** avoid anything **negative** about the **other parent** to the child. That way they are more apt to tell you when something is bothering them, knowing you will not criticize that parent.

Practice active listening skills. "You feel _____ because _____" (e.g., "You feel sad because I hurt your feelings when I told you that you are always late for everything").

Develop Parenting Skills to Improve Your Family Life:

Take a **parenting** or child-development **class.**

Enter individual therapy to find the **causes of your behavior** toward your own child. I find that parents either try to do things exactly the opposite of how they were parented or fall into the dysfunctional habits of their parents.

Provide **individual therapy** for your child and participate in family therapy.

Be kind to yourself. Use **positive affirmations** on a regular basis. Negative patterns, beliefs, and behaviors can be changed. Be aware of what you are doing and saying.

Find a time during the week to have a **family meeting** where each child and parent can express things that bother them without negative ramifications; make it a safe time to **work out problems**.

Admit when you make mistakes and ask for feedback from your child about how they would like you to do or say something (instead of the way you did it).

Speak about **your needs** and have them understand that communication in the relationship is very important.

You have a **right to your boundaries** and the child needs them. **Consistent fair** boundaries keep them feeling safe and secure. Be firm and loving.

Quick Win Strategies:

- Understand the effects of emotional abuse.

- Take a parenting skills class.

- Learn to communicate and set limits in a healthy way.

- Provide therapy for the child, yourself, and/or your family.

- Believe that change is possible and that it is worth the work you put into it.

Chapter 9
Eating Disorders

Do you have a child who overeats or has poor eating habits?

Is emotional eating a habit of a child you know?

Does your child refuse to eat or starve herself because she wants to be skinny?

Is your teenager showing signs of bulimia by hiding her behavior from you?

Are you looking for a way to help your child whom you suspect has an eating disorder?

Is your teenager's weight fluctuating more than normal?

Three Major Types of Eating Disorders:

Children and adolescents can develop eating disorders, which fall into three categories: compulsive overeating, anorexia nervosa, and bulimia. Children who overeat may be "stuffing" their emotions, utilizing being "big" as a defense or protection. If children are inactive, they are more apt to be overweight, which we are seeing more often in our culture. Those with anorexia basically eat as little as possible in order to look a certain way; they are starving themselves. Usually those with anorexia have an unrealistic sense of their body image and are perfectionists. They want a sense of control when they feel they don't have any. Many emotional factors drive this behavior as well. Bulimics engage in self-induced vomiting or use of laxatives after they eat high quantities of high-caloric foods because they want a way to gain control. However, the purging is highly detrimental to their health.

Warning Signs of an Eating Disorder:

Anorexia: skip meals, exercise obsessively, think they are fat when actually thin

Bulimia: go to the washroom after meals for long periods of time, eat healthy during the day and binge at night, have problems with their teeth and health

Compulsive overeating: binge eating of fatty or sugary foods, feel constantly hungry, eat when full

Emotional Eating

Children often use food as a way to self-soothe. If they have emotions that they cannot share with anyone, they stuff their feelings and eat to feel better. Sometimes this is a family pattern. I see it also as a society pattern. One of the goals I have for writing this book is to bring to everyone's attention that expressing our feelings is essential to our overall health. That is why I have included sections on communication for parents. The more we express ourselves, the less likely we are to depend on food for relief. Children also gain weight to protect themselves emotionally, perhaps from others around them. Children and adolescents who have been sexually abused often have an eating disorder to mask the pain inside.

Case Study

Sometimes children do not know why they are overeating. Their unconscious/subconscious mind drives them to overeat. What that means is that they have had a past experience where the lack of food was so profound that their body remembers the trauma of starving. That memory of starving goes to the survival pattern. In order to survive, the body feels it needs to eat. It is still hungry, famished even. That past experience could be in this life or in a past life that circles around in their unconscious like a recorded message. What I do is help the child bring that memory to their conscious mind by using my storytelling technique. It is uncanny how once the children tell these stories and release the feelings attached to them, the pattern dissipates and they do not feel the compulsion anymore.

Such is the situation of a girl I saw in therapy that I am calling Nicole who came to see me when she was six years old. She had a loving family and enjoyed being with her older sisters all the time. Her parents brought her to me because, not only was she always hungry, craving food and putting on extra weight, but she would also cry a lot for no apparent reason. She wouldn't sit still. She had to be actively doing something or she would get anxious. She wanted to be the center of attention constantly and had a way of bulldozing her needs first in the family. She never liked to be without someone around and would nag her mother when there was any downtime. Her parents were worried about her overeating, so when she entered therapy with me, they made a nutritional change in the whole family's diet as well.

I started working with Nicole around her constant hunger issues, using my storytelling technique to help her find where that need was coming from. I started a session by asking her what it felt like when she hadn't eaten for a while. She said, "It feels bad. I'm hungry." Then I asked her, "If somebody was hungry in a story from a long time ago, would they be alone or with other people?" Nicole responded, "Other people." We started to make some people figures out of clay, and I continued to ask her questions. As I pointed to a figure, I asked, "Who is this person?" She answered, "It is a girl, and she's wearing a funny scarf." I asked, "What are these people feeling that we have made out of clay?" She answered, "Hungry."

I continued the story in another session because young children often cannot stay with a story as long as an older child. I asked Nicole if she could speak for the girl in the funny scarf as we re-enacted the story in the sand tray, and she said she could. "When you don't get food right away, what do you feel?" I asked the girl figure in the sand-tray scene. "I'm starving," she said. "What is the worst thing that could happen if someone is starving?" I asked. "Die," she said. "That is very scary. Is there anything else that is happening that is scary?" I asked. "They are scared they will lose somebody," she responded. "Does the girl lose somebody?" I asked. "A man takes the mom away. She is gone and the girl feels sad," she answered. I asked her what she wanted to do with the man who took her mother away, and she said she wanted to make him out of clay and pound him. I use this technique to help the child express her anger at the "bad man" (as she called him), to help release the pain and memory, and to externalize the internal pain—to get it out of her.

My focus was to take the physical hunger that plagued Nicole and see if there was unconscious material that was driving that hunger. I felt that she was telling me a story about the Holocaust. However, at no time did I mention that word. In my many years of experience doing past-life regression with adults, I have worked with people who were in the Holocaust in a past life. The signs of hunger and separation from family are issues common to those who experienced being in a concentration camp in World War II. The issues that Nicole was dealing with in the here and now and the past were the feeling of continuous hunger and not wanting to be separated from her family. It wasn't my job to prove that she had been in the Holocaust. My job was to make sure I had cleared all the issues that may have been stemming from that experience. Believing in past lives was irrelevant to her healing process. In another session she told me that her whole family was gone. She lost them all. "Some people came and gave her candy and got her out. The girl was very sad and lonely," she told me.

Nicole has a lovely personality with a strong character that always shone through with anything she did with me. Some people argue that children are closer to the experience of past lives, so it is easier for them to reconnect to those experiences. They haven't spent years denying and repressing memories. I think this may have been true about Nicole. She was able to express her emotions.

Nicole and I continued to discover another lifetime that was negatively affecting her. It related to her anxiety in this life, her loneliness when her sisters weren't around, and the boredom she felt when she didn't have something to do. She had been a servant in a household who worked constantly and was afraid she would put something in the wrong place or she would forget to do something. As a servant girl, she was tired but couldn't stop working. She needed to be constantly on the move much like how she felt inside herself when she was bored. Feeling the sadness and loneliness of this lifetime released the pain inside her and helped her healing process.

As a result of our work, Nicole was able to tolerate being by herself and working on her own. Her anxiety went away, and she was more relaxed and at ease in different situations. With her family's help nutritionally, Nicole regained a normal weight and no longer had the obsession to eat. She has a great sense of humor and is a joy to her family. On one of her last sessions, she said, "I went to the principal's office because my skirt was too short. After the principal told me not to wear short skirts, I told him, 'You are probably going to see a lot of me in your office this year!' He was speechless."

Eating Disorders in Adolescents:

When working with teenagers who have eating disorders, I have found that there is a psychological cause that drives this behavior. Symptoms that accompany the eating disorder include low self-esteem, helplessness that comes out as control issues (i.e., when we are helpless, we do not have control), depression, and anxiety. Sometimes the unconscious patterns and beliefs are creating the behavior. I clear those patterns and beliefs from wherever they are coming from in the past. Those adolescents with eating disorders do not feel that they can speak what is truly going on inside them. When any of us do not speak our truth, we find maladaptive behaviors to hide the confusion and pain inside us. It is no different for adolescents. They are trying to find a way to control their body when the world is a place where they do not feel control.

This next case is about an adolescent with an eating disorder and other issues. She had no knowledge of why she had the behaviors she did, but by the end of the session, she was clear of the past. I have tried to give more detail about what was said to give you a better picture of how I work and the importance of finding past lives, bringing them back into memory so that our unconscious mind can problem solve an ancient pain.

Case Study

A couple years ago I was fortunate enough to be able to give a presentation to a large group of past-life therapists, students, and alternative health professionals at a conference in India. As part of the talk, I wanted to give a demonstration so that the audience could see what I do "live." Then during one of the breaks, a family came up to me: a mother, father, daughter, and son. They said that they had come to the conference because they wanted their thirteen-year-old daughter to meet with me while I was at the conference so that I could conduct a session with her. As I spoke to the young girl about her fears, I asked her if she would be willing to be the demonstration for the conference. Though she was shy and unsure, I encouraged her. I told her that these adults needed to know how to work with children in a different way to make a difference in the world. She thought about it for a while and then agreed.

When talking to Chanda and her parents, I found out that Chanda was a very picky eater. She barely ate at meals. She said she had these "little fears" and did not like people to force her to do things. Her self-concept was low, and she did not think she was smart or capable. Though she had a loving family, she was not close to her father. In fact, since birth she would not even get near her father. She also had a lot of anxiety around studying and doing her homework. Chanda and her parents believed in past lives, so I could work directly with her in that way.

As the demonstration was about to begin, we sat together at a table with mounds of clay on a stage in front us. The adults were either sitting on the floor or in chairs in the audience. I asked her if we could use the clay together, and she agreed. However, the clay was very sticky. It had been used previously, and a lot of water had been added to the clay. She did not like the stickiness but was a good sport and followed my directions. I asked her to take a piece of clay, stand up with me, and throw the clay down on the table, making a big sound. When she threw the clay down, it slipped out of her hands and landed in the audience. As you might imagine, this brought great roars of laughter from the audience. We tried it again. Sometimes it would land on the table and other times in the audience. This brought all kinds of giggles from Chanda and the whole room. I asked her to say how she felt about the clay while she was throwing it. She said, "I hate this sticky clay." Her nervousness about being in front of a crowd began to disappear as she physically and verbally expressed herself. I threw the clay right along with her and repeated her words as a way for her to feel I was supporting and validating her. Children find strength when I partner with them in the experience.

I used this technique of throwing, ripping, and tearing the clay to help Chanda release some anger and to allow the clay to help facilitate the session. Clay has magical qualities that bring out astounding experiences for both children and adults. It is hard to describe unless you have experienced it yourself. When I train therapists to do my work, I always give them a piece of clay to practice my technique. Countless times those adults have had breakthroughs with the aid of the clay. It has a way of putting a person in an altered state of consciousness, much like right before one goes to sleep, and helps them to access past experiences and emotions.

Then Chanda and I began by making figures out of clay to re-enact the past experience. We talked about how she felt about being forced to do things she does not want to do, and I used that as an opening to the session. I began by asking her, "If there was a story from a long time ago of somebody who was forcing you to do something that you didn't want to do, what is the first thing that comes to mind that they would be forcing you to do?" She answered, "Marriage." This word just popped out of her mouth. It surprises people how quickly these words coming from the unconscious can appear. I then asked her, "How do you feel when you are forced to marry this person?" while I point to a clay figure I made.

I often make figures of people with clay to enable the child to "see" in front of her the re-enactment of the story. She answered, "He is stupid. He is a bastard!" I found out later that these were not words Chanda used at home. It was not in her vocabulary in this life. Those words were coming from another lifetime. I continued to ask her questions. I pointed to a figure I had made of her and the man, and I asked, "What do you want to say to this man?" She answered, with a lot of anger, "I don't want to get married. But there is no other way," she added with more of a sad tone in her voice. I asked her how she felt about being forced to marry this man. "Deeply hurt," she said. "Is there anything you can do about it?" I asked. "I cannot speak against my father because he would treat me very badly," she said. "What does that feel like if you speak up knowing they will treat you very badly?" I asked. "I am deeply hurt and feel like I want to die," she answered. I told her how horrible this was for her. I went on to tell her that she lived in a culture in that lifetime where the rules were so strong and she was helpless to do anything about it. Past-life stories bring up emotions that the child is not aware she has, and I validate those feelings for her. People are taken aback when they first have a past-life regression session—that emotions so easily appear—and Chanda was no exception.

In the next part of the session, I asked her to tell me about the marriage. She went on to tell me that the husband mistreated her. She said that he was a womanizer (again a word her mother said she had never used in this lifetime) who abused her when he was drunk by hitting, slapping, and kicking her, all the while telling her that she was useless, a coward, stupid, and a fool. I asked her how it felt to be abused like that, and she said, "It feels like my life is over. I am useless because I cannot stop him from doing those things to me." At this point Chanda believed the husband because she was helpless to change him. I interceded by creating more figures out of clay. As I pointed to them, I asked her, "You can't stop him because you have how many people telling you he can do whatever he wants?" She answered, "Everyone." I asked, "So how can you do anything to stop him?" She answered, "I can't." This powerless feeling has kept her locked into the false belief that she is not capable or smart.

We went on in the session as I asked her what finally happened in the marriage. She told me, "He runs away with another woman and no one cares about me. I feel alone." I asked, "Over time, what starts to happen to you?" She said, "I am sad and alone." I asked, "What finally happens to you in that life?" She responded, "I die." I asked, "What brings about your death?" She said, "Hunger. I didn't get any food or anything to drink for many days because they believe that it is all my fault."

In most sessions with children and adolescents, they go to the part of the lifetime where they die. The death becomes a crucial boundary, i.e., the point where there is an end to the suffering. As an adolescent Chandra was able to move through this death with my help. I told her, "Go to the part where you start to die, where you are hungry." She folded down into herself as her body was feeling the pain. I asked her, "What do you want to say?" She told me, "I want food. My stomach hurts. I want people to help me. I want to do something very good, but

I can't. I am useless." I asked, "Who made you believe that you were useless?" She said, "My husband and my stupid father."

Some people may ask if it is appropriate for an adolescent to feel a death; maybe he/she won't be able to handle it? The way I handle it is by telling the children, "When we are born, we start our life, and when we die, it is the end of our life. It is sad, but all stories of people's lives end with death." I often ask families if they have spoken to their child about death and what their beliefs are about death. When I talk to children about death, I include the beliefs of that family.

This is the point of Chanda's session where I wanted her to get her power back, to externalize her internal pain. So we took all the figures of clay, punched them and squashed them, and I had her use her words to tell the truth. She said to the figures: "You are an idiot. You are so mean and foolish. Your rules of marriage are stupid."

Finally, I asked her to make herself out of clay and to tell me about herself in that life and in this one. She said, "I wanted to help people. Now I want to become a doctor." Both her parents are doctors. I asked her, "What kind of qualities would you need to become a doctor?" She said, "Patience, be smart, fast and kind." I asked, "Are any of those qualities foolish? Were you really foolish is that life?" She said, "No, I wasn't foolish. I wasn't a coward. I wasn't stupid." I asked, "Was there anything in that life that you learned that might help you now?" She said, "I will understand people better. It will help me figure out the characters and know if I can trust people or not." I asked, "Have you been able to trust people in this life?" She said, "No, I mean yes, but I think I will know more when I get older." I asked, "What do you want to tell me about your figure of yourself?" She said, with a smile on her face, "She is kind and beautiful." I asked, "Are you in a family that would force you to go into a marriage?" She said, "No." I stated, "So you have come into a family where you get to be who you are." She answered proudly, "Yes." I thanked her for her courage to share that day.

This ending to the session is called reframing. It means that I help the child delete the beliefs of the past and "own" who she is today. She is sloughing off the old patterns of being in a kind of starvation mode that has created her picky eating style and her low self-esteem around being smart and capable by clarifying who she really is today in her own words.

What happened after this session was astounding, almost like a miracle. Following this session we all went to lunch. My friends and colleagues at the conference came up to me so excited and told me that not only was Chanda eating her food with relish, but she was leaning against her father in a loving way. Later the family came up to me with tears in their eyes, telling me how grateful they were. It was a beautiful thing. Chanda said she did not feel afraid anymore and had a big smile on her face. I had many people come up to me following this demonstration telling me how they loved my work and appreciated what they saw.

Her mother followed up a few years later by stating:

> I am full of gratitude from Past life [sic] Research Conference, held three years back at Hyderabad, India. It was a life changing conference for my daughter,

121

who was regressed by madam Christine Alisa with clay therapy. Madam Christine Alisa helped her to go into a trans [sic] and speak about the past live [sic] experiences, which was [sic] blocking her in present life at academics. It was removed by madam Christine through Regression Therapy [sic]. K.S.V.

Body Image:

Body image refers to what the child/adolescent believes about how they look, their appearance. It includes how they feel in their body—comfortable or uncomfortable. Children, who have a distorted perception of their body and its shape, including parts they do not like, have a negative body image. They often feel ashamed or self-conscious about their body. There is an awkwardness in their bodies, all the while they are comparing themselves to what they believe is the "ideal" body. Mary Pipher, PhD, describes in her book *Reviving Ophelia* what happens to girls as they enter puberty. She states, "As their bodies change they "surrender their relaxed attitudes toward their body and take up the burden of self-criticism."

Certainly the culture, movies, advertising, and peer pressure contribute to the anxieties that children start to have about their own bodies. According to the National Eating Disorders Organization, "Those who have a negative body image have a greater likelihood of developing an eating disorder and are more likely to suffer from feelings of depression, isolation, low self-esteem and obsessions with weight loss."

Louise L. Hay has written about daily positive affirmations and how they can change how you perceive yourself. One of her exercises is called "mirroring." It is when you look in the mirror and say positive affirmations to yourself, such as, "I deserve to have/or be _____ (slender, healthy, like my body), and I accept it now." How do you feel? What is going on in your body? Do you feel unworthy? If you have any negative feelings about your body, try another affirmation. She suggests, "I release the pattern in my consciousness that is creating resistance to any good. I deserve to _____ (be happy with my body)." Repeating these affirmations is part of her holistic philosophy that has helped people heal. *You Can Heal Your Life, 86–88.*

Solutions:

Communication Strategies

Plan how you are going to **talk to your child**. Be gentle yet concerned. Tell him/her that you have **noticed** some **changes** in their behavior, and you need to talk about it.

Be prepared that your child may not want to talk but encourage them to anyway.

Eating disorders can **affect a child's health**, so treat it like you would if they had a **disease or illness** and you needed to take them to a doctor or alternative health professional.

Talk to your child about **peer pressure** and **body image**. Just **listen**. Avoid giving advice or solutions when you are listening. **Ask them** if they want some **advice** at the end.

Share some of **your emotions around eating** with your child as well. Don't "dump" your issues; just share a feeling. You can be a role model so that your child can feel freer to share his/her own feelings.

Create times to have **family conversations** where whatever is said will not be admonished; create a safe place to share.

What to do if you suspect your child/ adolescent has an eating disorder:

Work with a nutritionist to create **healthy meal plans** for the whole family. This takes a lot of time and energy. Ask your child/teen to help you find healthy foods as you shop **together** and plan meals together.

Teach your adolescent to prepare healthy snacks and foods for their lunches.

Have your child **write** down in a **journal** the feelings that come up when they want to **overeat, binge, vomit, or skip meals** completely. Make sure the journal is confidential.

Talk to a friend or spouse about the feelings that come up for you. Having a child/adolescent with an eating disorder can make you feel **powerless and fearful** and you need a place to vent your emotions.

Eating disorders can occur because of **family dynamics**. Are you part of the problem? Then the whole family needs to be involved. Seek a **qualified therapist** who **specializes in eating disorders** or treatment center for your adolescent, depending on the severity of the disorder.

Be **aware of any changes** in your child/adolescent's behavior around food or meals. Speak to a doctor or **health professional** to find out if there is anything physically wrong with your child.

Introduce your child/adolescent to positive affirmations. Tell your child how you **love them** just the way they are. Tell your child that his/her body is unique and that is a good thing.

Have them share what **pressures** they are feeling **from peers** around eating. Do not let them hide what is going on inside them. Listen and be supportive.

Quick Win Strategies:

- Notice if your child is showing signs of an eating disorder.

- Take action by consulting a health professional and therapist.

- Change some of your habits at home to empower yourself and your child.

- Open the lines of communication with your child/ adolescent.

- Change negative beliefs to positive ones by changing your language.

Chapter 10
Attention Deficit Disorder, ADD, ADHD

Does your child become distracted easily and find focusing difficult?

Is your child fidgety, wanting to move around instead of sitting still?

Has a teacher or doctor recommended medication for your child?

Are you against medicating your child and worried about the side effects?

Is your child/adolescent having problems with school performance?

Are you looking for an alternative approach to helping your child with ADD or ADHD?

Definition of the diagnosis according to the DSM-5:

As a therapist I am required to use the *Diagnostic and Statistical Manual of Mental Disorders – 5* to diagnose children. I include the explanation of the diagnosis for your information:

> The essential feature of attention-deficit/ hyperactivity disorder (ADHD) is a persistent pattern of inattention and/or hyperactivity-impulsivity that interferes with functioning or development. Inattention manifests behaviorally in ADHD as wandering off task, lacking persistence, having difficulty sustaining focus, and being disorganized and is not due to defiance or lack of comprehension. Hyperactivity refers to excessive motor activity when it is not appropriate, or excessive fidgeting, tapping, or talkativeness.

Common Medications, Statistics, and Side Effects

Mainstream or allopathic medicine, as homeopathic doctors call it, prescribes various stimulant medications for children diagnosed with ADD or ADHD. They include Ritalin, Adderall, and Concerta. Common side effects of these stimulants are difficulty sleeping, irritability, headaches, loss of appetite, upset stomach, depression, and tics. According to helpguide.org, "These side effects also differ from child to child, for some, they far outweigh the benefits."

Dr. Tom Insel, NIMH director reports, "The latest estimate from the National Center for Health Statistics reports that 7.5 percent of U.S. children between ages 6 and 17 were taking medication for 'emotional or behavioral difficulties' in 2011-2012." According to Dr. Insel , "The CDC reports 'a five-fold increase in the number of children under 18 on psychostimulants from 1988-1994 to 2007–2010, with the most recent rate of 4.2 percent.'"

Medicating Children: A Controversial Subject

A well-known psychiatrist by the name of Dr. Peter Breggin has written extensively about ADD, ADHD, and the negative effects of medicating children in his book *Toxic Psychiatry and Medication Madness* as well as in his many other books and journal articles. He states:

> The time is past when the focus in mental health was on what drugs to take for what disorders. Now we need to focus on how to stop taking psychiatric drugs and to replace them with more person-centered, empathic approaches. The goal is no longer drug maintenance and stagnation; the goal is recovery and achieving well being [sic].

He goes on to say, "So-called ADHD children are not receiving sufficient attention from their fathers." He says the real diagnosis should be DADD or dad attention deficit disorder. He says that these children are just more spirited and energetic than other children. He sees children with behaviors that look like ADD or ADHD as just in need of a more interesting environment, and he does not see it as a mental illness.

Alternatives to Medication

Many parents are seeking alternatives to medication through diet, herbs, vitamins, supplements, minerals, fish oil, and homeopathy. Others are providing neurofeedback, massage, Reiki, chiropractic and/or relaxation techniques, or emotional freedom technique, otherwise called "tapping" for their children. Parents are seeking to find a new solution without the harmful reactions in their children. Alternative practitioners—whether they be naturopaths, homeopaths, energy workers, or therapists like myself—are providing healing solutions to many of these searchers.

I believe it is time to radically change our attitudes toward ADD and ADHD. We, as advocates for our children, need to take action to free the child from the debilitating label and subsequent problems of these diagnoses. In my experience, children with ADD or ADHD symptoms have emotional concerns. Many of these emotional issues stem from the family and can be improved with psychotherapy and education. Other origins of these emotional conflicts can originate in past lives.

How I Work with ADD and ADHD:

In the years that I have observed children who have been diagnosed with ADD or ADHD, I have discovered some common issues. Many of these children have experiences in the past that have created the symptoms and behaviors that we find in this diagnosis. When children have difficulty sitting still or their minds won't stay still enough to focus, they are caught in some stuck place. What that means is that something traumatic has happened when they were not able to move or get away from a difficult experience or place. That place may be a difficult birth, prenatal trauma, early childhood trauma, or a past life.

As we know, our stress pattern is based on fight or flight. We want to get away from something that is causing discomfort, fear, or danger. We cannot always fight our way out of things, which leaves only one other solution—fleeing the scene. If they are constantly on the move, then they are safe. When children are distracted, they are trying to get away from the unconscious issues that are bothering them. Children are just trying to be safe. In my office, when children uncover past experiences where they were stuck, helpless, and could not escape a difficult situation, they are finding the causes of their need to move. Then the need to move is less compulsive, and healthy habits can restore the child.

Another characteristic that I find when working with ADD or ADHD children is the disconnect they have with their own bodies. It is like they are not totally in their bodies. They may "space out," as if they are not really there or they do not know where their edges are—they do not know where their bodies begin and end. They bump into things or energetically bump into people.

One of the goals that I have for therapy with children is that they be able to identify their feelings that are attached to difficult experiences. Children are very close to their emotions, more so than adults. They experience emotions that sometimes overwhelm them, and they don't know how to deal with them. Developmentally, we know that babies' brains have a developed amygdala where their root feelings are located. However, they have not developed cognitive functioning, which helps them "think" through their needs. They cry and then their needs are met. Children's brains are developing, but their emotions are still very intense. When events in their lives have brought about intense emotions, they need to express them aloud without judgment from adults. If, however, these emotions are not expressed verbally, they find other ways to come up, usually in the form of behaviors. So getting children to feel things and express them in a safe environment enables them to use an alternative to misbehavior.

Shamanism is another alternative healing technique that is helpful for children diagnosed with ADD and ADHD. In the next case studies you will learn how I incorporated my therapeutic model of therapy and skills as a shamanic practitioner into the restorative work I did with children and their families.

Case Study

Vicki was diagnosed with ADHD when she was seven years old. Her grandmother, who was her legal guardian, did not want to medicate her and chose therapy instead. The school system gave Vicki extra services because she was diagnosed ADHD, which many schools provide. Vicki had trouble remembering things she had just learned, and she constantly "spaced out" in the classroom.

Vicki came from a family of addiction, neglect, and abuse where she was expected to take care of her younger siblings. She was removed from the home because of those problems and went to live with her grandmother. In a session where she re-experienced an episode of abuse by her father, she told me that her father threw a bottle at her, which hit her head. I guided her through the breath process, breathing out shock and dizziness. Emotional shock kept Vicki safe during the violent attack, but it was now keeping her unconscious of her past. I had Vicki breathe to get her to clear cells of the attack. I helped her dislodge the words that her father was yelling at her. He was calling her "dumb" and "stupid." As she told me these things, I stood near her and used my hands above her head to literally "pull out" these words, the dizziness, and the pain. I was pulling out the negative energy inside her head. This is part of the shamanic technique called extraction. I now use shamanic principles with children and adults in my private practice where it is appropriate.

Vicki would avoid listening to anybody. Her unconscious belief was that if she could block out everyone else, maybe she could block out her father as well. In her attempt to achieve what she couldn't safely do with her dad, she disconnected from everyone else. She didn't listen to her teacher, which hindered her ability to concentrate. This distractible behavior was her attempt to get away from the trauma, but it also kept her from being attentive in class.

One place where a child is stuck and cannot get away from anything traumatic is the womb during the prenatal experience. One day in therapy we drew pictures of when she was inside her mom. I asked her, "How do you feel inside Mom?" She answered, "Stuck, trapped."

I continued, "What is happening that is making you feel stuck and trapped?" She said, "My dad is hitting my mom and saying bad words. He is calling her a stupid bitch." I asked her, "How do you feel, hearing him say that and hit your mom?" Vicki replied, "I feel scared and sad." I said, "When you are feeling scared, sad, and trapped, what are you afraid Dad will do to Mom?" She responded, "Kill her." This overpowering fear coincided with her own fear that her father was going to kill her. I moved her into her birth so that she could feel disconnected from this trauma and breathe on her own. We did a rebirth together and the stuck feeling was released. She felt freer because the rebirth changes the survival pattern: I have to feel afraid and trapped in order to be alive.

Vicki was able to express all her feelings of anger and hurt and how she learned to shut down or "space out" as a way to get away from her father. By the end of therapy, she was concentrating better in school. She was at grade level or above in her subjects, and she was feeling pride about her achievements. She was feeling her "true self": the feisty, funny girl she really was. Much of her distractibility was her need to get away from all her feelings originating with her early childhood. We did a lot of anger work to help her through that process.

Case Study: Cassidy and Her Family

I have the privilege of being able to work with families and to witness the remarkable, radical changes that occur with each member. Such is the case of Cassidy, her stepmother, and father. I choose to share their personal story with their permission because it illustrates the profound abilities that people have to restore themselves and create fluid harmony with each other.

Cassidy was an eleven-year-old girl who came from a family of addiction and divorce. Her father gained custody of Cassidy when her mother was actively abusing drugs and alcohol. Cassidy lived primarily with her mother and father until she was six years old, but her mother was the one who was primarily at home with Cassidy in her formative years. Cassidy's stepmother and father had previously brought Cassidy to several therapists with no positive results. They interviewed me to find out about regression therapy to see if it might be effective for Cassidy. I explained my therapeutic process, and they agreed to have Cassidy see me for therapy. At that time the parents gave me a history of Cassidy's early childhood and her current lack of a relationship with her mother. Her mother had been ordered by the court to have only monitored visits with Cassidy, but she refrained from paying for those visits and had not seen Cassidy for several years.

Cassidy had been diagnosed with ADHD, depression, anxiety, impulsivity, and compulsivity. She had trouble with control—both inner and outer control. I began to use my regression therapy techniques to uncover a desolate and chaos-ridden early childhood. We found that not only did her mother not want her when she was pregnant and birthed Cassidy, her mother actively neglected her during her formative years. There were many times when Cassidy was left to her own devices as a toddler while her mom was passed out on the couch. This lack of contact created a void inside Cassidy and a confused idea of herself. She lacked love except from her father. He was a recovering addict and was functioning higher than the mother, but he didn't know how to consistently be there for his daughter.

I bring up Cassidy's case because so many families are plagued in some way with addiction, and the effects of that addiction create symptoms and behaviors in a child. Cassidy ended up displacing her anger toward her mother onto her stepmother. She shut down her feelings so much that she had an almost impenetrable wall set up between her and anyone else who tried to get close. We worked together to find the places where she felt the sadness, feeling stuck, and helplessness of her early life and used my anger and feeling-release techniques to reduce some pain. I also utilized my shamanic practices to release a spirit that was attached to Cassidy. The parents also had a spirit that was attached to Cassidy's bedroom removed.

When I work with children, I always include the families. I often recommend that the parents see me individually to help them clear the negative dynamics that contribute to the child's dysfunctional behavior. Being willing to dig down deep into the reservoirs of each parent's past along with opening their world to a more spiritual connection through the practice of shamanism gave this family the strength that they needed to rebuild their family relationships. Both parents were able to have negative spirit attachments detach from their bodies and energy fields. Cassidy's father told me after his session with me, "It felt like there was more room inside me." After clearing his past-life issues, he regained his empathetic self and was a more patient, calm parent and husband. The parents' marriage had been moving toward divorce, but they turned the corner and now have a close relationship bonded with more love for each other than ever before.

I told Cassidy that she was the catalyst that helped restore her family. Steadily, her attention deficit disorder improved, but her oppositional, defiant behavior needed to be addressed in a more structured setting than I could provide as a private practice therapist. She was referred to a wilderness program and in an equine treatment program. Cassidy had a great deal of difficulty with empathy for others. She had a "mask" that covered who she truly was. It provided a wall of protection. She is now making progress in many areas. Sometimes private practice therapists cannot do everything to help a child who has gone through such terrible deprivation. I am grateful for the programs that truly help adolescents and their families. We are continuing our work together with the family to heal the wounds and bring them closer together.

Solutions:

Communication Strategies:

Spend **one-on-one** time with your child and listen to them. **Do not say** things like, "Why don't you ever listen?" or "Think before you act," or "Pay attention."

Ask them, "What can you do to shift your energy right now?"

Be **firm and clear** about your behavior expectations and be **consistent** with your **limits**.

Be **empathetic** with your child. i.e. "I understand you are frustrated at school."

Listen to, **acknowledge**, and accept the child/adolescent's **stressful feelings**.

Allow them to brainstorm some **problem solving techniques** they can use, thus giving them a part in the solution.

Suggestions for Parents to Help Their Child Diagnosed with ADD/ADHD:

Give your child lots of loving **attention** and **attend to yourself** as well.

Help them **shift their energy** by getting in the water/ pool, a shower or participating in a calming activity.

When **doing homework**, be creative. Such as let them **manipulate** something in their hands while they concentrate, **have fun** and laugh together, take breaks to stand up and move around, stop for a **quick game** together and then get back to the assignment.

Provide **interesting creative activities** for your child, ones that he/she likes.

Give your child opportunities for **one-on-one time** with yourself and other loving adults.

Provide your child with **hands-on activities**, such as art, crafts, drama, and pet care.

Be respectful to your child. Do **not raise your voice** in anger or frustration.

Allow your child to be more **'spirited,'** so they utilize their energy.

Provide clear **daily routines** and **structure**.

Provide **clear rules/boundaries** and stick to them.

Provide plenty of outdoors **exercise** for your child.

Speak to your child's **teachers** about how to provide extra **movement** in the classroom and **tactile** experiences that are **not disruptive**.

Refrain from labeling your child to your child or others.

Investigate a smaller school or **smaller classrooms** where he/she will receive more attention.

If there have been some stressful experiences in your child's life, provide **therapy** for him/her with a **qualified therapist**.

Try some simple **meditation**/relaxation techniques with your child.

Explore **dietary** changes and **alternative remedies**.

Consider **alternative healing** modalities, such as massage or Reiki.

Participate in **family therapy** and self care for yourself so you can re-energize.

Recap of the Solution for Quick Action:

- Explore alternatives to medicating your child.

- Provide a loving, structured environment with open communication.

- Be an advocate for your child with the schools.

- Provide therapy and alternative healing techniques for your child.

- Participate in family and individual therapy to heal your own wounds.

BONUS: To hear some **practical** tips in calming your child so they can **successfully focus** and **finish** their homework, watch my video on **3 Tips to Helping Your ADHD Child.**

To receive this BONUS CONTENT please go to this link:

http://christinealisa.com/WPBook.html

Chapter 11
Traditional vs. Nontraditional Therapies

Are you confused about what is traditional and what is nontraditional therapy?

Are you interested in finding a therapist that works traditionally with children?

Would you like to understand more about what nontraditional therapy is?

Would you like pointers for finding a nontraditional therapist for your child?

As I draw to a close in this book, I would like to clarify for parents the difference between traditional and nontraditional therapy with children and adolescents.

The primary form of therapy today is traditional. One type of traditional therapy is called play therapy. You can check this out at *a4pt.org* for more information. The goal of these therapists is to use play therapy techniques to help the child communicate and respond better to the world. They are a national organization with lists of therapists in different parts of the country, and they provide ongoing training for therapists.

Another commonly used traditional therapy is called evidenced-based therapy practices, which involves cognitive and behavior therapy (CBT). Their website is *abct.org*, and you can learn more about their approach there.

Gestalt therapy with children and adolescents as developed by Dr. Violet Oaklander is another traditional approach, and you can find out more about her at *vsof. org*. Though she no longer has a private practice, she does have books and materials for your edification. Each of these modalities specializes in a particular therapeutic format, but they all focus on helping the child.

Nontraditional therapies include my own storytelling process that I conduct with children and adolescents, and you can find more information about that on my website at *peacethroughmetamorphosis.com.* As you have discovered, I have a clinical background in traditional therapy, but I have added past-life regression and shamanic healing techniques to my practice, which makes it nontraditional. One of my colleagues, Carol Bowman (*carolbowman.com*) is also a highly respected past-life therapist who has written an excellent book called *Children's Past Lives.* Her work is also nontraditional.

There are many qualified therapists who conduct past-life regression sessions, and you can find one at *ibrt. org* or at *earth-association.org*. Many healers such as Reiki Masters, body workers and energy healers also contribute to the world in a non-traditional manner. Their gifts play a big part in the healing process of children and their families and I invite parents to utilize their talents so we treat the whole child deeply and successfully.

For more information about shamanism, check out *shamansociety.org/organizations.html*.

There are many books available on both these healing modalities, and I invite you to learn more about these empowering techniques for our children and our own mental health and well-being.

My vision is to see a world without abuse and my purpose is to create a platform of healers to make that change possible. Whether you are a healer, parent, educator or therapist and you feel called to be a part of my movement, I welcome your reactions, comments and suggestions about this book and look forward to hearing from you. Let us make a difference in children's lives and let us do it together.

Bibliography

"Abraham Maslow." *Abraham Maslow.* Copyright 1998, 2006 by C. George Boeree, n.d. Web. 13 Sept. 2015. <http://webspace.ship.edu/cgboer/maslow.html>.

Alisa, Christine, MS. *Turning the Hourglass: Children's Passage through Traumas and past Lives. S.l.:* Authorhouse, 2012. Print.

Association for Play Therapy. N.p., n.d. Web. <http://www.a4pt.org.>.

"Auditory Processing Disorder." *KidsHealth.* Ed. Thierry Morlet. The Nemours Foundation, 01 Sept. 2014. Web. 13 Sept. 2015.

<http://kidshealth.org/parent/medical/ears/central_auditory.html>.

Breggin, Peter, MD, and Ginger Ross Breggin. "Psychiatric Drug Facts with Dr. Peter Breggin - The Hazards of Treating ADHD with Ritalin." *Psychiatric Drug Facts with Dr. Peter Breggin - The Hazards of Treating ADHD with Ritalin.* The Journal of College Student Psychotherapy, Vol. 10(2) 1995, Pp. 55-72, 1995. Web. <http://breggin.com/index.php?option=com_content&task=view&id=123>.

"Child Abuse Statistics." *Childhelp Child Abuse Statistics Comments.* N.p., n.d. Web. 13 Sept. 2015. <https://www.childhelp.org/child-abuse-statistics/>.

"Childhood Obesity Facts." *Centers for Disease Control and Prevention.* Centers for Disease Control and Prevention, 19 June 2015. Web. <http://www.cdc.gov/obesity/data/childhood.html>.

"Emotional Abuse." *NSPCC.* N.p., n.d. Web. 13 Sept. 2015. <http://www.nspcc.org.uk/preventing-abuse/child-abuse-and-neglect/emotional-abuse/>.

Farber, Adele, and Elaine Mazlish. *Talk So Your Teen Will Listen and Listen so Your Teen Will Talk.* N.p.: Collins, n.d. Print.

Farmer, Steven. *Earth Magic: Ancient Shamanic Wisdom for Healing Yourself, Others, and the Planet.* Carlsbad, CA: Hay House, 2009. 221. Print.

Finkelhor, David. "Welcome to the National Center for Victims of Crime." *Welcome to the National*

Center for Victims of Crime. N.p., n.d. Web. 13 Sept. 2015. <http://www.victimsofcrime.org/>.

Freedman, Joshua. "The Physics of Emotion: Candace Pert on Feeling Go(o)d • Six Seconds." *Six Seconds.* N.p., 26 Jan. 2007. Web. 13 Sept. 2015. <http://www.6seconds.org/2007/01/26/the-physics-of-emotion-candace-pert-on-feeling-good/>.

Hay, Louise L. "P. 86-88." *You Can Heal Your Life.* Santa Monica, CA: Hay House, 1987. N. pag. Print.

"Home » Earth Association." *Earth Association.* N.p., n.d. Web. 14 Sept. 2015. <http://www.earth-association.org./>.

http://peacethroughmetamorphosis.com. N.p., n.d. Web. <http://peacethroughmetamorphosis.com>.

http://www.a4pt.org. N.p., n.d. Web. <http://www.a4pt.org.>.

http://www.abct.org,. N.p., n.d. Web. <http://www.abct.org,>.

Insel, Tom, MD. "Director's Blog: Are Children Overmedicated?" *NIMH RSS.* Tom Insel, M.D., 06 June 2014. Web. <http://www.nimh.nih.gov/about/director/2014/are-children-overmedicated.shtml>.

"International Board for Regression Therapy." *International Board for Regression Therapy.*

N.p., n.d. Web. 14 Sept. 2015. <http://www.ibrt. org/>.

Irlen, Helen. *Irlen*. The Irlen Institute, n.d. Web. 13 Sept. 2015. <http://irlen.com/>.

"Neurodevelopmental Disorders." *Diagnostic and Statistical Manual of Mental Disorders, Fifth Edition*. Washington, DC: American PsychiatricPublisher, 2013. 61. Print.

N.p., n.d. Web. 13 Sept. 2015. <http://www.apa.org/ topics/trauma/>.

N.p., n.d. Web. <http://www.shamansociety.org/ organizations.html.>.

Oaklander, Violet. "Chapter 10, Pg.280-282." *Windows to Our Children: A Gestalt Therapy Approach to Children and Adolescents*. Moab, UT: Real People, 1978. N. pag. Print.

"Optometric Extension Program Foundation." *Find an Optometrist*. N.p., n.d. Web. 13 Sept. 2015. <http://www.oepf.org/page/map>.

"Optometric Extension Program Foundation." *Find an Optometrist*. Optometric Extension Program Foundation, n.d. Web. 13 Sept. 2015. <http:// www.oepf.org/page/map>.

Ortner, Nick. *The Tapping Solution: A Revolutionary System for Stress-free Living*. Carlsbad, CA: Hay House, 2013. Print.

"Past Life Regression Therapy and Children's Past Lives
- Carol Bowman Past Lives." *Carol Bowman Past
Lives*. N.p., n.d. Web. 14 Sept. 2015. <http://
www.carolbowman.com/>.

Paul, Thomas, and Morris Netherton. "Netherton
Method Past Life Therapy-Past Life Regression."
Netherton Method Past Life Therapy. Past
Life Therapy Center, 2013. Web. 13 Sept. 2015.
<http://www.pastlifetherapycenter.com/
TheNethertonMethod.html>.

Pipher, Mary Bray. "Pg. 57." *Reviving Ophelia: Saving
the Selves of Adolescent Girls*. New York:
Putnam, 1994. N. pag. Print.

"The Relationship Between Sexual Abuse and Risky
Sexual Behavior Among Adolescent Boys: A
Meta-Analysis Cited in Scopus: 15 Yuko Homma,
Naren Wang, Elizabeth Saewyc, Nand Kishor
Journal of Adolescent Health, Vol. 51, Issue 1,
P18–24 Published Online: March 6 2012." N.p.,
n.d. Web. <http://www.nim.gov/medlineplus/
news/fullstory_123919.html>.

"Statistics About Diabetes." *American Diabetes
Association*. N.p., 18 May 2015. Web. <http://
www.diabetes.org/diabetes-basics/statistics/.>.

"Systematic Biology Volume 64, Number 1 January 2015
- Front Cover." *Systematic Biology* 64.1 (2014):
I1. Web.

"Violet Solomon Oaklander Foundation." *Violet
Solomon Oaklander Foundation*. N.p., n.d. Web.
14 Sept. 2015. <http://vsof.org./>.

"What Is Body Image? | National Eating Disorders Association." *What Is Body Image? | National Eating Disorders Association.* N.p., n.d. Web. 14 Sept. 2015. <https://www.nationaleatingdisorders.org/what-body-image>.

"Why Play?" *Play Therapy Makes a Difference.* N.p., n.d. Web. 13 Sept. 2015. <http://www.a4pt.org/?page=PTMakesADifference>.

Www.nationalchildrenalliance.org. N.p., n.d. Web. <http://www.nationalchildrensalliance.org/media-room/media-kit/national-statistics-child-abuse.>.

About Christine Alisa

Christine Alisa, MS, is both a traditionally based clinician and an alternative therapist. She is a creative innovator who helps people through crisis of meaning and radical transformation. She uses her powerful intuitive wisdom and empathic and problem-solving skills to help adults, children, adolescents, and their families move through powerful integration and resolution. As a spiritual teacher she facilitates past-life regression and shamanic healing practices that provide guidance and tools to enhance and empower others through life's challenges. She is an international speaker and trainer of therapists, bringing her therapeutic work she has developed for children and adolescents around the world. Christine has written two other books: *Turning the Hourglass: Children's Passage Through Traumas and Past Lives* and *Your Amazing Itty Bitty Book on Communicating with Your Teenager.* She is a marriage family therapist, past-life therapist, and shamanic practitioner who has been in private practice for over twenty-five years in Southern California. Her business is called Peace Through Metamorphosis, and she is a member of several organizations, including the California Association of Marriage Family Therapists, the International Association of Regression Therapists, The Earth Association for Regression Therapy, the Association for Regression and Reincarnation Research, and The Association for Play Therapy.

"Enjoyment, fun, knowledge, patience, compassion, deep love ... those are the observations from Regression Therapy workshops of Christine Alisa. We need to heal our inner children for a better future. We need to heal

*our inner child to have complete and integrated souls.
That is why what Chris is doing is really crucial work."*

*- Tulin Etyemez Schimberg,
Unicorn Transformational Studies, Turkey.*

Connect with the Author

You can find out more about Christine Alisa at:
www.peacethroughmetamorphosis.com

Please connect with Christine Alisa on
Facebook and Twitter:

Two Facebook Pages:
Peace Through Metamorphosis and christine.alisa.5

Twitter: @ChrisAlisa_MS

Or e-mail her at: chris@christinealisa.com

Gratitude and Acknowledgements

I want to take the opportunity to thank all those who have taught me, encouraged me, supported and nudged me along my journey. I appreciate all the training and knowledge I gained early on from my friend, Dr. Violet Oaklander, whose dynamic work has been spread all over the globe. Thanks go to my first past-life therapy teacher, Dr. Morris Netherton, for giving me a format to build upon; to the many organizations that have allowed me to speak on their stages; and to the many healers, shamanic practitioners, and energy workers who have shared their expertise with me.

My deep appreciation extends to all the children that have touched my heart in so many ways and to those who are represented in this book. Having the opportunity to "be" with another soul as a witness as they uncover their deep layers leading to wholeness has been a profound gift for me. I am very grateful to the parents who have trusted me with their children and have walked the path of growth to attain more fulfilling lives.

To Dennis Merkley for his tireless support keeping me afloat while proofreading; to Brianna Merkley for showering me with so much love; to my massage therapist, Samantha Marcella, who saved my hands from carpel tunnel; to my friend Dr. Susan Fisher for her emotional support; to Mimi Donaldson who said "Do it!"; and to my many spirit guides who support and love me from the other side, I extend my heartfelt thankfulness.

Special gratitude goes to Robbin Simons and her Crescendo Publishing Company for giving me a structure to shape my message so that it may be more accessible to those who are seeking a different road of healing for their children. Robbin's encouragement and creative genius have given me a vehicle to communicate to a wider audience the material that is a gateway to my larger purpose in this lifetime.

www.ingramcontent.com/pod-product-compliance
Lightning Source LLC
Chambersburg PA
CBHW060928040426
42445CB00011B/839